CHANGING DIMENSIONS OF LIBRARY AND INFORMATION SCIENCE

CHANGING DIMENSIONS OF LIBRARY AND INFORMATION SCIENCE

P.S.G. Kumar

Ess Ess Publications
New Delhi

Changing Dimensions of Library and Information Science

ISBN: 978-81-7000-714-2

₹ 995/-

First Published 2014

Published by:
Ess Ess Publications
4831/24, Ansari Road,
Darya Ganj,
New Delhi-110 002
INDIA
Phones: 23260807, 41563444
Fax: 41563334
E-mail: info@essessreference.com
www.essessreference.com

Cover Design by *Patch Creative Unit*

Printed and bound in India at Salasar Imaging Systems.

To
My Grand Children
Omkar Vihan
&
Minakshi

Contents

TYPES OF LIBRARIES

Public

School

College

Preface

I has the opportunity to participate in over 160 conferences and seminars; delivering 192 lectures; and giving over 80 keynote addresses, etc. Most of them were structured and published in special seminar volumes and a few in professional journals. The rest of the talks were extempore.

The themes of my talks were varied, covering a wide spectrum; and presenting the current trends in the subject. It is in this context , I thought it proper to put text of these talks together in one volume so that it would be comprehensive and handy to an average professional.

The Unit 1 starts with a general discussion on the problems and consequences of higher education in India *vis-a-vis* libraries. The other subjects in this unit includes the catching-up phrase 'Learning Resource Centre'; language barrier in communication; designing skills programme for users; etc.

The second unit gives an insight to some of the fundamentals of the profession, its philosophy and ethics.

The third unit comprehends the ICT and its impact on libraries. The articles in this unit provides an insight into technological environment in libraries. It comprehends articles on computerization, planning automation, history of technology in libraries with a stant to India, electronic resources, services, etc.

The Unit four comprehends issues specific to kinds of libraries — public, school, and college. About public libraries, it pinpoints to issues like legislation, community, information, etc. Under school libraries Ranganathan's 'Library Centrad Education' was discussed in detail. The two talks on college libraries stresses on the need for reengineering.

The fifth unit touches upon the areas like information literacy, management techniques, quality in libraries, innovation, etc.

Thus, this collection provides an insight to new developments in the field which are changing the dimensions of the discipline continually and for the better.

I am sure, readers will have a good go through in this volume.

Hyderabad

P.S.G. Kumar

GENERAL CONCEPTS

1

Changing Context of Higher Education and Libraries*

INTRODUCTION

Chief guest of today's function Prof. Y. Venkatarami Reddy; Director of the seminar Dr. E. Rama Reddy; Mrs. Kameswari, Principal, Govt. City College; Dr. G. Sujatha, Chairman, FALA; Dr. G. Narasimha Murthy, Organising Secretary FALA Conference; distinguished invitees and fellow librarians -I am indeed grateful to the organizers for inviting me to deliver the key-note address at this national seminar on a very relevant topic.

Facts

There are two important facts of the theme of the seminar:

* Keynote Address delivered at FALA (Federation of Academic Librarians' Association) conference held at Hyderbad between 10-11- Sep. 2005.

1. Changing contexts of higher education; and
2. Challenges for the librarians

Objectives

I would like to modify the objectives laid-down by the organizers in the following fashion:

1. To note the changes in higher education;
2. Impact of changes in higher education on libraries and their services; and
3. To evolve integration of new trends in higher education with library services.

CHANGES IN HIGHER EDUCATION

The Changes in higher education can be seen as

1. Environmental changes
2. Administrative changes
3. Academic changes
4. Technological changes

Environmental Changes

Intensive to Mass Education: Earlier the students use to go in search of a good teacher. These days the teachers have to search for a good student. Teaching was individualized as well as intensive. Today ours is a mass education, as a result, there is no proper attention on student.

Guided to Self Education: When the objective is to have mass education, teacher is not in a position to pay needed attention on the student. The student cannot totally depend on class-room teaching. Either he has to depend on tuition classes or on self-study.

Ideal to Money Making: Earlier educational institutions were established with noble ideals and mainly of charity. These days education has been commercialized and the objective of starting an educational institution is to make money.

Administrative Changes

Earlier government was the major supporter of education. With increase in the need for mass-based education, a large number of private institutions have come-up.

Mass Production of Graduates: Almost for the last 150 years, if there is any thing static, it is only the educational system. We are producing the same graduates - in arts, sciences and commerce. This is the reason why one of our professionals described the process as "manufacturing the graduates but not producing them".

More Quantity - Less Quality: Quantity and quality are inversely proportional. As quantity (extension) increases, quality (intension) decreases. Pupil is coming out today with less knowledge and skills. As such they were found to be misfits in the job market.

Cheaper to Costly: Education is becoming costly day by day. This is on two counts: 1) Decreasing support from governments; and 2) increasing commercialization.

Academic Changes

Academic Changes include: (1) Stagnant syllabus; (2) Less interaction between the teacher and the taught; (3) Easy examination system ; and (4) Notes and Guides - based education.

Stagnant Syllabus: It is observed that the syllabi of most of courses at various universities seldom change. The books prescribed for the study of various subjects are mostly those published in 1950's and 1960's. Though subjects are growing at a rapid rate, it is taking a long-time to enter the courses.

Less interaction between teacher and the taught: It is unfortunate that the attendance of students in the class is very less. In some colleges it is almost zero. The interaction between the teachers and students is almost nil. Thus, the basic purpose of education is defeated.

Easy Examination System: The examination system is also contributing to its might for the falling standards of education. The same questions are repeated alternatively and students' preparation for the examination by mastering a few questions will easily get through the examination.

Notes and Guides based Education: Most of the students confine to the class notes given by the teachers. They found it sufficient to get through the examination and get respectable score. It is said in lighter vein the notes given in most cases is the one the teacher got when he was a student. Further, a lot of guides, question - answer works are available in the market, which are written exclusively to meet the examination requirements of the students.

Technological Changes

With the development of global information networks; online retrieval of information; interactive video systems; computer simulations; new storage and transportation media, etc., a good lot of changes have occurred in the field of education.

Virtual Campuses: It is said that we are going to have virtual campuses-leading to 'one world : one university'. Cross border education, migration and collaboration of universities; online learning; tele-teaching and tele-education will have greater impact in the years to come.

Globalisation: Education is becoming globalised. There is an increase in cooperation, collaboration and interaction among the universities.

There are certain advantages and disadvantages of these developments. Advantages are getting up-to-date knowledge; continuous monitoring and evaluation of the courses, etc. Whereas, disadvantages include lesser practical training; more or less becoming a one way process; and the cost of education is going to be higher.

CHANGES NEEDED IN HIGHER EDUCATION IN INDIA

1. Higher Education should be a subject of the Union government;
2. The medium of education should be:
   (a) Elementary education - mother tongue
   (b) Secondary education - mother tongue & English
   (c) Higher education - English only.
3. There should be more interaction and exchange of the faculty. This could be possible when union government takes up the responsibility of higher education and the medium of instruction is English.
4. Syllabus should be continually updated and if necessary teachers should be trained in imparting new concepts. There should be more debate at national level with regard to contents.
5. New developments in educational and information technology like teaching aids, information retrieval, teleconferencing, interactive learning, use of multimedia etc., should be exploited to the extent possible.
6. Existing information networks should be used to the fullest extent and new networks should be developed. Global networks should also be put to the best advantage.
7. Traditional courses be replaced gradually with new courses, covering new branches of knowledge.
8. Apart from NAAC, there should be independent agencies for monitoring, structuring and evaluation of courses.
9. Education should be made free from politicalisation.

LIBRARIES AND HIGHER EDUCATION

Though several educational committees and commissions described library as 'heart' of an educational institution; center for lifelong, perpetual and self-education; etc, the situation is quite different and pathetic. The organizers are right when they said that "the library system in higher education is reduced to a mere decorative piece; the library is not well articulated in many aspects of academic and administrative governance; and the library is characterized by "growth without development".

Changes Needed

The well rounded development of a library and effective library services depend on the trinity - management, authority and library staff.

The following factors make or mar good library services.

1. Proper funding of libraries.
2. Free hand to librarians to plan and executive the library system;
3. Library centered teaching; where the teachers make the students to use library books by giving references, assignments, projects, group discussions, etc.
4. New educational and information technology should be adopted in libraries. Library staff should continually keep an eye on the developments in these fields - particularly the concept of 'paperless society'; 'Library without Walls'; Tele - education, impact of tele-commuting etc.
5. Library staff should draft special training programmes for teachers and students in retrieval and use of information.
6. Looking to the diverse roles to be played by library staff as navigators of information; nettisonions;

facilitators of information; packaging of information, innovators of new information products and services. We all have to rise to the occasion and accept the challenges with challenge.

I am sure, we will be able to meet the challenges with dedication, devotion and determination.

I thank the organizers for calling me to do this job. Thanks to every one of you for your patient listening.

2

Learning Resource Centre: Concept and Scope*

FROM LIBRARY TO LEARNING RESOURCE CENTRE

The traditional library aims at collection, processing, organization, and dissemination of information in traditional sources like books, journals, etc. In a traditional library a user is expected to come to the library for use of documents. Lending of certain class of material for home-use is also allowed.

Technological developments made it possible to reach-out to the users beyond the four walls of the library. A variety of non-book material started reaching the libraries. Initially, it was microforms-microfilm, micro-fische, and micro-card. Then came audio material like wire recordings, discs, tapes

* Address delivered at the Programme on "Libraries as Learning Resource Centres" at Mahila Mahavidyalaya, Nagpur on 5 Dec. 2009.

etc. These days, video tapes, discs, etc are common forms of recording and disseminating of information.

A library in an academic institution, is designated as a 'Learning Resource Centre' which is a blend of traditional book oriented library service and multimedia services. A 'Learning Resource Centre (LRC), not only disseminate the information to the teachers, students and scholars, but also helps teaching-learning process in an academic institution by going to the class-room.

MY AMERICAN EXPERIENCE

I had an opportunity to visit typical LRC at Tulsa Junior College (Oklahoma, USA). All the in-house operations like cataloguing, circulation, serial control, etc. are fully computerized.

OPAC

The Online Public Access Catalogue (OPAC, is kept in the entrance of the library, close to public service personnel work station. The OPAC answers queries by the name of the author, title as well as subject. The entries are arranged alphabetically. Approaches, by joint authors, alternative titles, etc. are also answered. Cross references are interspersed through out indexes. The location symbol consists of 'type of material' (media, motion picture, etc) and LC class number.

Circulation

Each user of the library is given an ID card with the help of which they can check-out library material.

Reserve Material

The LRC with the assistance of the teacher segregates books, magazines, articles and other materials useful for class assignments, and are kept on 'Reserve.' The students can easily complete their class-room assignments with the help of the materials placed on reserve.

A few reference books and some current high interest titles are placed on permanent reserve by the LRC.

Orientation

Three kinds of orientation programmes are regularly carried out by the LRC.

1. Orientation Tours : Emphasizes locations, services, policies, and introduction to staff members;

2. LRC Instruction : Class related lecture tours highlighting resources useful for specific assignments; and

3. Bibliographic Instruction : Discussions and exercises related to key research tools and their uses. Presentations are tailored to the needs of the group, and may extend to several sessions.

News Bulletin

The LRC maintains a continuing electronic 'Bulletin Board' system (BBS)' detailing the news, policies and events related to the institution as well as LRC. Important notices are also displayed on their system. The BBS also includes a list of some of the television programmes of academic interest available via satellite.

Periodicals

A list of complete holdings, their format and location are on the index table. List of periodicals on a subject is available on request.

Current issues of journals are kept on display shelves. They are filed alphabetically by title. Newspaper 'trees' hold daily and weekly newspapers.

These days, hard copy forms are being replaced by electronic formats. Bibliographic databases are available on CD format. Consortia and national networks are in position to provide quick and cheap access to literature in electronic forms.

Reference and Referral Service

Users are encouraged to suggest titles of books for purchase. Reference collection is available for use. Reference Librarian on duty helps in seeking answers to questions, using reference works., and indexes and finding needed material. Inter-Library Loan from local libraries is arranged.

A number of folders containing newspaper clippings, and pamphlets are housed in vertical files, and kept near the reference desk.

Bibliographic searching through databases on national and international networks is provided, of course, at a price.

Coin operated copy machines are available for student use.

A small circulating collection of career books giving information about career opportunities, job requirements, conditions and rewards is maintained. PCs are available free of charge, for the use of students.

MEDIA SERVICES

Multimedia hardware and software are available, for class-room use and for use in LRC. Advance booking is necessary in view of heavy demand. Media equipment is made available with one day notice.

Closed Circuit Television (CCTV)

In order to facilitate services to media class room needs, a CCTV system has been installed and thirty-six rooms are equipped with monitors and control panels. Faculty members are encouraged to use this system when they are planning to show a film, or videotape. With this system, there is no need to set-up and operate a projector, no unwanted noise from the projector, and light can be kept on for note-taking. If it is a monitor equipped classroom, the teacher can directly contact CC room simply by picking up the telephone receiver of the control panel in the class-room.

Telecourse Viewing

Telecourse tapes are available for review by students on video-tape machines. Now-a-days, CD is one of the best media for recording and dissemination.

Graphic Area

In the graphic area a wide range of material like slides, original photographs, overhead transparencies, original art works, filmstrip, duplication, charts, posters, graphs, layouts for publication etc., can be provided.

Production Guide

This area provides many production related media services. These include off-air taping of cable programming, video-production of lectures, meetings, speeches, and special presentations, audio production, video duplication and audio duplication.

CONCLUSION

Thus LRC can not only provide traditional library services, but also help making teaching more effective, learner oriented, bring live displays to the class-room and make learning quick and enjoyable.

3

Language As a Barrier in Communication of Information*

CONCEPT OF INFORMATION

The word 'Information' comes from the Latin word *informare* meaning to inform, or *give to* (my italics); and the *Oxford English Dictionary* gives 1387 as the first date in which the word was used in its English form. For some years this was mainly within the context of religious teaching, but in 1450 there is an example of the use of the word to mean "knowledge communicated concerning some particular fact, subject or event; that of which one is apprised or told; intelligence news". This later definition brings in the word knowledge,, and in the year 2005 we still tend, unhelpfully, to use the terms interchangeably. The classic work, by the

---

* Keynote Address delivered at the State Level Seminar on "Language and Communication" held at G S Patil - Munghate College, Dhanora (MS).

Japanese authors Ikijuro Nonaka and Hirotaki Takeuchi *(The knowledge-creating company)* introduced the concepts of tacit knowledge and explicit knowledge (i.e. information in its librarian' sense). So, information remains a tangible resource to be managed, while knowledge is an intangible resource to be captured.

There is growing acceptance among senior executives of the vital importance of information and knowledge in a post-industrial society, but a poor understanding of these abstract resources that can be re-used over and over again, but on which it is impossible to put a price. We need books written from different viewpoints, before we can claim to be master of the information revolution. We should remember that the theory of steam power came after the invention of the steam-driven locomotive.

The observation or behavioural constraints state that the concept of information must explain and predict observed behaviour of individuals (or knowledge structures), with respect to information. Three observations are particularly striking in these instances, and have been much discussed. They are: the differences of responses of different individuals to the same data, the differences of response of the same individual to the same data at different times, and the differences of response of the same individual to the same data presented in varying forms. For "differences in response" one could substitute "varying effect". The first two observations I would like to group together into a single constraint, which is that the informational effect of a particular set of data varies according to the state of knowledge of the recipients. Or, as others have put it, that information is seen as a *change* in state of knowledge.

NATURAL CHARACTERISTICS

Exponential Growth

Since the invention of printing, there has been a

continuous revolution in the generation, transfer and communication of information. Information, infact has been growing at an exponential rate which is often referred to as "Information explosion". Information is carried and communicated through various media. These can broadly be categorised into two — the 'documentary media', and the non-documentary media'. In the documentary media, book production more than doubled in a decade. Presently more than 10,000 titles are published every working day and thus, more than 3 million in a year. The production of periodicals rose from 10,000 titles in 1900 A.D. to 170,000 titles in 1971 A.D.

Doubling of Knowledge

According to American National Education Association:

"It took until 1750 for man's knowledge at the time of Christ to double. The second doubling was completed 150 years later in 1900. The fourth doubling of all man's knowledge took place in the decade of 1950s. Looked at another way, technology has multiplied by 10 every 50 years for over 2,800 years. In 1950 there were one million scientists and engineers in the world; in 1900 there were 100,000; in 1850-10,000; and in 1800-1,000."

According to Rider — American libraries which try to collect everything appearing on a given subject double their size every 16 years.

Information is Cumulative

Gathering of Information

Human activity can be viewed as a process of building-up of knowledge. The knowledge is built-up in two ways — individually and collectively. The knowledge conserved by human, we call "Universe of Knowledge'. The individual knowledge is the sum-total of ideas comprehended by a person. An individual gathers information either by (sensory) experience or through formal education or by both.

Storing Information

The knowledge acquired by an individual is stored in his brain or in material form by recording the ideas using a medium. The retention of ideas in human mind will depend upon the frequency of application, interpretation and use. The recorded information can be retrieved at any time without missing any of the item stored. Further, recorded information will be available for wider public use and is subject to interpretation.

Application

The information available can be elaborated, consolidated, interpreted and used for varied purposes basing on the kind of information.

In Research and Development

Impact of Information Explosion

Mr. Weinberg in his report to White House submitted in 1963 stated that :

"We shall cope with the information explosion in the long run only if some scientists and engineers are prepared to commit themselves deeply to the job of sifting, reviewing and synthesizing information, i.e. handling information with sophistication and meaning not merely mechanically. Such scientists must create new science and not just shufile documents : their activities or reviewing, writing books, criticizing and synthesizing are as much a part of science as is traditional research."

Aslib carried out a survey on the impact of information on R & D in 1960s. The response from 245 R & D personnel was analysed as follows :

	Finding	Number of Responses
(a)	Information made available in dicated duplication of the work of others	43
(b)	Information, had it been known earlier would have led to :	
	(i) Planning the research differently	36
	(ii) Alter the plan of research in progress	60
	(iii) Saving of time, money and research potential	106

Wastage of Resources for Want of Timely Information

UK : The estimated cost of unintended duplication in scientific research in UK due to delay in the supply of information in the 1960s was Rs. 21.6 million.

USA : The estimated annual cost by way of unintended duplication of governmental research in the field of electronics in the sixties was Rs. 15 million.

The estimated cost of 5 years of research on electronic translation equipment in USA proved to be duplicating the work already done and published in Russia was Rs. 18.7 million.

According to a report of the Controller General of US, the US Airforce and NASA spent a whole year inadvertently developing similar space vehicles – Atlas Agena B and Atlas Vega. This costed a wastage of Rs. 135 million.

Informational Pollution

With the increase in the volume of information, it is becoming difficult to locate and pull out specific information. Special Assistant to the President of USA stated in 1965 that:

"Chaos, duplication and waste are the words used more and more frequently by responsible members of our nation's scientific community to describe the problem they face in being unable to refer effectively to the records of the previous accomplishments."

J.D. Bernal long back stated that: "It may be easier to find out a fact by experiment or to build-up a theory than to ascertain from the published documents whether these have been discovered or deduced before."

The explosion of literature does not really indicate the growth of new ideas. According to Bourgeois, Former Director, National Library (Switzerland) "out of 100 technical articles only 8 furnished a really original contribution to learning and research."

Need for Free Flow of Information

Free flow of information, from its generation to the ultimate consumer, has been a subject of concern to librarians, documentalists, scientists and of late to - governments also. It is of immediate concern to scientists, authors etc. who are the ultimate consumers. Strangely enough, scientists who are the primary generators of information, in turn become the consumers also. Between them the information flows in a sort of cyclical continuum. "Information is both a major nutrient and a primary end-product of research and development. The information utilized by the scientist can be considered as "input" to the research effort, and that resulting from their work as "output". Thus a feed-back has to be organized and maintained with the least amount of dissipation and wasteful duplication, so that the flow of information is streamlined and automatic.

In a wider perspective, the information or the knowledge which concerns society at large, and which alone makes individuals well-informed and able to judge and discriminate, has to be organized so that there is not only an unhindered free flow but freedom and right to its access is also guaranteed.

Information equally needs free flow across national ideological, political and language barriers. In the field of developmental activities, it is said that inadequate information alone is costing one billion dollars a year resulting in development funds being wasted, to say nothing of even more important loss of energy and opportunity and hope, or of resulting extension of human suffering.

Barriers to Communication

The barriers to communication of information can broadly be grouped into the following categories:

(a) Institutional impediments;

(b) Financial;

(c) Technical;

(d) Linguistic;

(e) Social and psychological; and

(f) Administrative and political.

Institutional Impediments

There are three basic institutional impediments. These are:

(i) Status (of a person and organisation)

(ii) Structure (Hierarchical); and

(iii) Secrecy (Fear of Losing).

Linguistic

"Language differences impose a barrier to all communication...," wrote Dan Lacy in *'Challenges to Librarianship'*. His thesis was that foreign language barrier is an impediment to the process of international understanding and consequently a threat to peace, progress and prosperity of the world—a view which has found acceptance everywhere. The diversity of languages throws a challenge to the world of librarianship also, for, we acquire, organise and disseminate information which cuts across the barriers of language differences.

Man's inherent instinct is to communicate his

experiences to his fellow beings. From gestures, signs, pictograms man has passed on to an epoch of symbolism and ideograms. Susanne K. Langer says that it is the power of using symbols that sets man so far above other animals. It is the power of speech that makes him lord of the earth. In other words, language is nothing but the highest developed form of symbolism. Ernst Cassirer, the famous philosopher remarks, "Language—the symbolization of thought—is man's prime instrument of reason." Language so far is the most effective tool of communication. Cassirer goes on to say, "Between the recepter system and the effecter system, which are to be found in all animal species, we find in man a third link which we may describe as the symbolic system. This new acquisition transforms the whole of human life. As compared with other animals, man lives not merely in a broader reality; he lives, so to speak, in a new dimension of reality."

In order to decipher the meaning of a particular symbol, we must know its key. Each language is also related to a particular community of men. Therefore, one learns from childhood the mother tongue. But one is not generally initiated to other languages prevalent in other societies. And thus we come across the 'language differences' referred to above by Dan Lacy and, we find ourselves imprisoned in the language of our society and culture.

"Inability to read any language other than one's own mother tongue means the loss of an ever-increasing amount of information, the ability to search for and find pertinent information on a subject is governed, to a great extent, by the language knowledge of the searcher." The appearance of materials relevant to all fields of knowledge in various languages is a sort of necessary evil. It is a phenomenon which, librarians will have to reckon with.

Though languages were ostensibly created to facilitate communication, quite often they become the major hindrance to the communication of scientific and technical information. Each linguistic community virtually forms an island by itself, in which only a few scientists can communicate with more than one or two other linguistic groups.

Initially, scientists thought that it will be sufficient for them, if they could master a few important foreign languages. Learning foreign languages formed part of education in science and technology. It worked well for some time. But, acceleration of research in hitherto regarded as minor linguistic groups, and library and information profession coming forward with organised translation services and bibliographic control of technical translations at various levels, changed the situation completely.

National and international documentation centres started maintaining permanent translators for all major languages. Panels of translators are being maintained by all documentation centres. Special training programmes are being organised for scientific and technical translators. Associations of professional translators are being formed in different countries. Apart from government sponsored agencies, commercial translation services have come up.

Exclusive translation centres at international and national level is a recent phenomenon. The European Translation Centre, 101 Deolestraat, Delft, The Netherlands is an example of international translation centres, which is concentrating on East European scientific and technical literature. Russian Science Information Centre at INSDOC supplies on demand English abstracts of Russian literature received in the centre. It also provides Russian translations.

Jargon: Even with a known language, there are problems associated with jargon, such as, neologism (= coining or using of new words); synonyms (= two or more words of the same language, with the same meaning but often with different implications and associations); acronyms (= word formed from the initial letters of a name, *e.g.* NASA); etc.

CONCLUSION

To Overcome the Barriers

Access to information is vital for the development of an individual, organisation or even a nation. Organisations should involve people at various levels in gathering pressing and utilisation of information for the benefit of the organisation.

Research and academic institutions should allocate reasonable amount of money for library and information units so that they can come out with suitable information.

4

Designing Skills Programme for Users*

SKILLS PROGRAMME

The following psychological principles have been identified by The National Council for the Social Studies as essential for undergirding a developmental study skills program:

1. The skill should be taught functionally, in the context of a topic of study, rather than as a separate exercise.
2. The learner must understand the meaning and purpose of the skill, and have motivation for developing.
3. The learner should be carefully supervised in his first attempts to apply the skill, so that he will form correct habits from the beginning.
4. The learner needs repeated opportunities to practice the skill, with immediate evaluation so that he knows where he has succeeded or failed in his performance.

---

* Text of a lecture delivered at Govt. D B Women's P G College, Raipur on 15 Dec 2008.

5. The learner needs individual help, through diagnostic measures and follow-up exercises, since not all members of any group learn at exactly the same rate or retain equal amounts of what they have learned.
6. Skill instruction should be presented at increasing levels of difficulty, moving from the simple to the more complex; the resulting growth in skills should be cumulative as the learner moves through school, with each level of instruction building on and reinforcing what has been taught previously,
7. Students should be helped, at each stage, to generalize the skills, by applying them in many and varied situations; in this way, maximum transfer of learning can be achieved.
8. The program of instruction should be sufficiently flexible to allow skills to be taught as they are needed by the learner; many skills should be developed concurrently.

A study skill, reference tool, and basic terminology continuum provides three levels of emphasis: (1) introducing the specific skill, tool, or term through planned experiences; (2) developing the skill and the use of tool or term within a context of functional utility and need; (3) reteaching, maintaining, and extending the skill or reference tool as part of the ongoing instructional program. The Appendix to the Thirty-Third Yearbook of the National Council for the Social Studies, *Skill Development in Social Studies* presents an excellent model of a comprehensive study skills continuum.

If a district study skills program has not been spelled out, then the librarians must take a leadership role in designing and implementing a plan for integrating learning how to use the library with the school's instructional programme. Florence Cleary, in *Blueprint for Better Reading: School Programs for Promoting Skill and Interest in Reading,* provides "Reading for Information and Knowledge," and "A Framework for Teaching the Investigative Skills," a step-by-step procedure to follow in organizing and implementing a library-based study skills program. It cleary suggests organizing instruction in the use of the library under the following categories:

I. Locational Skills

The supplementary skills for locating information that should be taught and retaught in high school include:

- Using library tools to locate books and other informational materials Locating ephemeral material through indexes;
- Gaining facility in the use of a number of special reference books in different subject fields—history, biography, literature, music, art, social science, science;
- Acquiring facility in the use of magazine indexes, such as *Reader's Guide to Periodical Literature,* and other specialized indexes as sources for locating current materials;
- Gaining acquaintance with all parts of the book: the title page, preface, introduction, table of contents, lists of maps and illustrations, notes, appendix, bibliography, and glossary;
- Learning about the arrangement and special features of dictionaries, encyclopedias, annuals, almanacs, yearbooks, atlases, and maps;
- Using special indexes of poetry, plays, costumes, essays, songs, and biography to find materials in collections;
- Acquiring ease in the use of handbooks, manuals, directories, and yearbooks for locating a variety of types of information; and
- Locating information from many sources and acquiring

essential skill in observing, listening, and viewing in order to obtain relevant information.

II. Selection and Organizational Skills

Regardless of the amount of emphasis given to skill development in the elementary and junior high school, the high school staff cannot assume that the pupils need no further guidance in selecting and organizing information. Instruction should continue, with emphasis on the following intermediate skills:

- Identifying the purposes for acquiring the information;
- Skimming to ascertain if the selection contains information pertinent to the problem;
- Choosing a number of important topics under which the information may be grouped;
- Selecting and classifying less important facts under the main topic;
- Examining large or major topics to determine the most systematic arrangement as they relate to the problem;
- Selecting all the facts that bear on the problem; and
- Jotting down sources of information and looking up unfamiliar words.

III. Interpretive Skills

A number of intermediate skills are basic to the interpretation of what is read:

- Understanding what the author means Relating and evaluating pertinent ideas;
- Evaluating the reliability of sources and recognizing and analyzing propaganda;
- Distinguishing between fact and opinion and recognizing and tracing pertinent relationships and time and place sequences; and

- Willingness to evaluate one's own attitude on the subject being examined.

IV. Generalizing and Conversion Skills

As instruction continues in the high school grades, there are numerous questions that teachers and librarians may use to give directions for reaching generalizations and conclusions and for evaluating decisions:

- What are the possible conclusions and generalizations which can be drawn from an analysis of the information?
- Have you taken into account your own biases and prejudices which might have influenced the reaching of these conclusions?
- Have you gone beyond your information in reaching conclusions?
- What do your conclusions indicate? Have they changed or clarified any of your previously held opinions or judgments?
- Can you use this information in making judgments and reaching decisions in other areas or with other problems?
- May further information make necessary a possible reconsideration of conclusions?
- Cleary identifies the abilities, facilities, and skills in locating and gathering information, in organizing, evaluating interpreting, and using information, and in reaching conclusions, solving problems, and sharing information. She groups these basic learning experiences under the following headings:

I. Getting Acquainted with the Sources of Information and Knowledge

Desirable learnings for pupils:

- Acquaintance with the many and varied sources of information
- Understanding of the skills involved in locating and gathering information
- Knowledge of the resources and services of the school library—as a vast source of information and knowledge
- Development of wholesome attitudes and habits in using the sources and resources of knowledge and appreciations

II. Acquiring Information and Knowledge Through the Skillful Use of Books

Desirable learnings for pupils:

- An understanding and appreciation of books as sources of information, as the record of man's cultural heritage and creative ideas and thoughts
- Knowledge of how books are written, illustrated, printed, published and distributed
- Appreciation of literary, aesthetic, and human values in books
- Acquaintance with books that provide for the enrichment and integration of the curriculum
- Knowledge of and facility in the use of the books as a source of information
- Facility in using such special features in books as graph, charts, illustrations, maps, and bibliographies

III. Locating Books and Other Learning Materials in the Library

Desirable learnings for pupils:

- Understanding of the opportunities for acquiring and utilizing knowledge through skillful use of books and libraries

- Knowledge of the various resources in the modern school library, and their location and use
- Acquaintance with and facility in using the Dewey Classification system in locating books on library shelves
- Skill in using the card catalog to locate books and other learning materials in the library
- Skill in the use of indexes and lists for locating poetry, plays, biography, short stories, songs, fiction, and other materials in collections
- Facility in locating films, filmstrips, records, flat pictures, and other audio-visual materials—those available in the school and those available through other agencies

IV. Locating and Using Current Materials

Desirable learnings for pupils:

- Understanding the value of current ephemeral materials as sources of information and knowledge
- Acquaintance with and facility in reading and using magazines as sources of information
- Skill in using magazine and newspaper indexes
- Facility in using and evaluating newspapers as sources of information
- Facility in using TV programs in documentary films as sources of information and knowledge

V. Using Reference Books to Locate Information

Desirable learnings for pupils:

- Acquaintance with and ability to use reference books that supply concise information about places, things, people, events and progress
- Ability to use general encyclopedias efficiently in gathering information

- Ability to use handbooks, almanacs, yearbooks, manuals, directories, and government and state documents in locating statistical information
- Ability to use appropriate reference books in securing information on special subjects and in special fields
- Facility in securing geographical information: location of place names, statistics concerning commerce, population, industry resources, and other pertinent data.

The above skills can be applied with advantage to any teaching-learning process.

5

Reference Service: Trends and Technology*

DEFINITION

The term "Reference Service' has been defined by Wyer as "the sympathetic and informed personal aid in interpreting library collection for study and research." Margaret Hutchins, on the other hand, defines it as "a service that includes the direct personal and within a library to persons in search of information for whatever purpose, and also various library activities especially aimed at making information as easily available as possible." A similar definition is given by Dr. Ranganathan, who states that 'Reference Service' is the process of establishing right contact between a reader and his document in a personal way.

* Keynote Address delivered at the National Workshop on 'Importance and Relevance of Reference Books and E-Resources for College Students' held on 6 Feb. 2010 at Dayanand Arya Kanya Mahavidyalaya, Nagpur.

FUNCTIONS OF THE REFERENCE SERVICE DEPARTMENT

The following functions are involved in Reference Services:

1. Answering the queries received from readers, either in person or over the phone or though correspondence.
2. Assisting readers in using library tools viz., catalogues and other references tools.
3. Preparing reading lists and ad hoc bibliographies on request or in anticipation.
4. Preparing guides to use the library and its collections.
5. Preparing special indexes and maintaining special files (e.g. Pamphlets, Newspaper Clippings etc.)
6. Providing selective dissemination of information to users.
7. Making arrangements for Inter - library loans, and if necessary inter-state or international borrowing.
8. Providing abstracting service.
9. Providing translation service.
10. Providing duplicating or copying facilities.

REFERENCE WORKS

The influence of reference works as a source of information has declined. The compilation of a reference work on a subject even on a limited subject is becoming almost impossible. One has to work with different authors and the whole operation is so extensive and time consuming that the work is obsolete before it appears.

There is a tendency to replace the large old fashioned reference books by monographs, books of more limited scope, on more specialised subjects. Monographs are not very different from reviews. There is rather a continuum, in that, monographs are based on the author's knowledge whereas reviews are based more on the literature.

A reference book thus treats a fairly large area of science systematically. Reference works are not generally meant for continuous reading. In a first approach to the literature on a subject, reference works cannot be missed. Reference work never goes deep enough into a subject and it never deals with latest literature. Reference works will be used only to tracing basic data.

NON CONVENTIONAL SOURCES

The non-conventional sources do not constitute a homogeneous group. Some of them are conventional documents in a non- conventional format and some are only media for communication or a system of communication. With the technological revolution we are not going to break away with the conventional packages, but, we are going to use them in tandem with the additional help of computers and internet.

The non - conventional sources need not reach a library and can be utilised without the help or control of the librarian. Thus, the librarian's role is unhelpfully restricted. According to Lancaster, "Electronic sources do not need to be selected, acquired, catalogued ...or bound...public service within the library can also be expected to decline. There will be no need to visit a library to borrow such materials." Thompson uses the term "data bridge" to cover electronic formats like Videotex systems, Videodiscs, full text systems, facsimile transmission, document delivery and electronic publishing. By this term he means, an information store which is directly accessible to the user without the need for a secondary source or guide, catalogue or index, or the need to obtain the item from a location at a distance by visiting a library which in turn may have to borrow the item from another location.

The technology has no doubt, bridged the gap between the user and the information source, but it cannot eliminate the librarian totally. Libraries are going to be there. The role of the librarian shall change. Information consolidation, liaison, referral service and user education are the jobs where librarian's role will be significant in the information age.

INTERNET

During 1969 the US Department of Defence, through their Advanced Research Project Agency (ARPA) created an experiment. This was a Packet Switched Network over telephone lines. Out of this initial network Advanced Research Project Agency Network (Arpanet) one of the early forerunners of Internet was born. During 1970s the ARPA developed a set of rules, called protocols, that helped in connecting different networks having different host computers. The number of networks connected to ARPANET continued to grow over the years. In 1982 ARPANET joined with MILNET (The Military Network) and a few others and it is said that the internet was thus formed from this consolidation of networks. As per the latest information available there are 2,20,000 current users on the Internet, and every month 1,50,000 new users are joining it. It is estimated that by the end of the year 2000 there were about 10 crore users and 10 lakh hosts on the Internet.

Services

1. Communication
2. Document or file transfer
3. Interactive browsing
4. Bulletin boards

Correspondingly to these activities there are four basic tools :

1. E-Mail - Electronic message exchange.

2. FTP (File Transfer Protocol) - moving electronic documents, images, sounds etc.
3. TELNET -accessing another computer system's database or archives.
4. USENET - global bulletin board service.

In addition to the above in later years some new tools have emerged that expand upon these four basic activities.

1. World Wide Web (WWW) - a hypertext interface to information on the internet.
2. Gopher - an information browser that lets us retrieve what we find.
3. Veronica - an enhancement to Gopher that searches many Gopher databases.

Video Discs

Videodiscs are becoming ultimate storage medium for information. It can contain text, sound and pictures - both still and moving. It can be passive or interactive and access to its information is random, unlike its predecessor video-cassette where access is sequential. Thus videodisc combines the advantages of the book with that of film, although there is the added cost of machinery for accessing the contents.

The mass storage available in limited space can make available the text of journals which are becoming increasingly expensive to publish and distribute to the user and to the publisher a reduction in photocopying of the journal and loss of revenue.

A later development wherein, a combination of videodisc and microcomputer provides automated journal reference system. The contents of one videodisc provide references to articles in over 1000 journals. Such is the power of this medium. This facility also reduced the need to hook-up to external online databases.

DIFFERENT KINDS OF OPTICAL/LASER DISCS

CD-ROM

Laser discs are one of read - only, write-once, or erasable and also one of analogue or digital. Read only optical or laser discs are expensive to produce and the data on the discs cannot be altered. These discs are suitable as a computer storage medium, specially when the information needs to be amended and updated. These are however suitable for electronic publication of documents and graphics. The read-only analogue version is useful for storing video images and can hold digital data by converting it to analogue data. The read - only digital disc has appeared in the form of CD and CD-ROM discs. A number of encyclopedias, dictionaries, collections of periodicals and other electronics documents are entering the market place in this medium.

Computer Software

Libraries use computer for providing access to information. Of late, many libraries in countries like UK and USA are providing computers and software for use on the premises. Libraries also play an important role in training users in the use of computers, assisting academic staff in developing courses in microcomputer applications and loaning the applications software.

Libraries are maintaining database of reference information. They are also providing access to external database through online facility.

Public started using the computers and software available in the public libraries in USA to calculate their entitlement to welfare benefits, tax assessment, and to manipulate data. A number of personalised information systems have become available in these libraries.

DIGITAL REFERENCE SERVICE

Since the early 1990s literature in library and

information science has considered the effects of the widespread use of the Internet on both reference practice and its resources. Around this time, the concept of "using the Internet as a resource to answer reference questions but also using the Internet to exchange information between patrons and librarians. Not long after, the Internet to exchange information between patrons and librarians. Public Library emerged as the case study for doing reference with the Internet for the interest community, making more clear the distinction between doing reference digitally (now called "digital reference") and using the Internet as a resource to answer reference questions in a traditional space. Ryan considers historically significant changes in information technology that have affected reference practice and notes that "the Internet is both the medium and the message," making the notion of "using the Internet for reference" still difficult to define.

In the mid -1990s reference librarians, understandably, continued to grapple with the use of the Internet among reference librarians and began discussions around the information of digital reference services in public and academic libraries. Research subsequently found digital reference services in slightly less than half of academic libraries and in about one in six public libraries. However, librarians are reportedly still not using free Web pages to answer reference questions, even when they are available. Additionally, when they speak to patrons about the Internet, it is often framed as "something that users might independently want to check out later on. Not surprisingly, research into "reference librarians' attitudes towards the World Wide Web" and toward "digital reference" continue to appear. As previously mentioned, recent discussions on digital reference have extended to include contemplation of commercial and non-commercial (but non-library) digital reference services, standards for digital reference projects, collaborative and real-time reference projects, and negotiating reference practice in the virtual space. Whether reporting a "confusing array of options" changing the look of reference or challenging reference librarians to "transform (reference) for the new age and prove their value" in order to merely survive, more than ever before, the phrase "using the Internet for reference" is loaded with energy, excitement, and even some anxiety about reference as an increasingly dynamic practice.

While obviously well positioned for serious and continued inquiry on many fronts, the relatively new arena of digital reference has revealed more questions than answers and continues to be considered by many as a novel area in reference, or at least one of dramatic change. The findings of this study continue to infer additional but similar questions ana to further develop ideas for continued research in digital reference practice and service.

With the text of journals held in electronic form it is natural that the next stage should be document delivery by electronic communication rather than by post, or personal travel.

With all these developments libraries will continue to be the principal point of interface between users and the collections being indexed or abstracted.

STUDENTS AS USERS

A study entitled "Students' use of the school library and attitude towards it" conducted by Brosman in technical school libraries in Melbourne, Australia provides the following findings.

(i) Most students visited the library in their spare time.

(ii) The large majority enjoyed the library, although the resources given varied considerably between schools.

(iii) Reasons for non-use included library restrictions and dislike of library staff.

(iv) Frequency of use and attitude towards the library differed from area to area and sex to sex.

(v) Boys visited the library more frequently than the girls and choose more non-fiction material and

(vi) There was no significant different in use or attitude between students with English speaking parents and those with non-English speaking parents.

USER EDUCATION

Librarians must take a leadership role in designing and implementing a plan for integrating learning how to use the library with the instructional programme in the college. A user education programme be worked out giving stress on :

1. Location skills:
2. Selection and organisational skills
3. Interpretive skills
4. Generalizing and conversion skills by :
   (i) Getting acquainted with the sources of information and knowledge.
   (ii) Acquiring information and knowledge through the skill for use.
   (iii) Locating Books and other learning material in the library. Locating and using current material in the library.
   (iv) Using reference tasks to locate information.

SOURCES USED

1. Grogan Denis, Grogan's case studies in reference work, v1 Enquiries and the reference process. London Bingley, 1981.

2. Guinchat, C. and Menou, M. General introduce to the techniques of information and documentation work. Paris, UNESCO, 1983.
3. James, Joseph and Hill, Chrystie. Finger on the pulse etc. (*Reference and user services quarterly* v42, N1; Fall 2002.p.55.
4. Kumar, P. S.G. Fundamentals of Information Science. Delhi : S. Chand, 1988.

BASICS

6

Library and Information Profession*

LIBRARIANSHIP TO INFORMATION SCIENCE

Traditionally there are three main branches in the profession—archivists, librarians and documentalists, within which certain specialisations such as bibliographer or indexer have become occupations in their own right. Today, however, people are more willing to accept that the information occupations all belong to a single profession. Before going into the details of the present information profession, let us look into some of the basic issues of our profession.

LIBRARIANSHIP—PROFESSION OK VOCATION?

There is a long standing dispute, whether librarianship is a profession or vocation. In order to resolve this, let us see what characterises a profession and as to what is vocation.

---

* Text of lecture delivered at Indirabai College of Library Science, Nagpur on 15 March, 1995.

Profession

A Profession warrants:

(a) A specialised knowledge of the field—scientific historical or scholarly;

(b) Intensive preparation for acquiring needed skills and methods to put the knowledge to work;

(c) A set of principles, a social code or ethics;

(d) An organisation that will bind all the numbers together for:

   (i) Concerted opinion.

   (ii) To achieve high standards in performance; and

   (iii) To act as force to achieve common good and work for collective thinking; and

(e) Working with the prime purpose of rendering a public service.

Vocation

A Vocation involves:

(a) An activity of some kind—routine, physical or scholarly;

(b) A craft, trade or profession:

(c) Need certain or no skills; and

(d) Mainly an activity involving service against fee or free.

LIBRARIANSHIP—A PROFESSION

From the above discussion we can safely conclude that librarianship is a profession rather than a vocation. Because:

(a) It needs a specialised knowledge—imparted in various library schools;

(b) It needs intensive training and continued practice *to* gain mastery over the skills needed for successful librarianship;

(c) A set of principles or professional ethics have been drawn;

(d) A large number of organisations at various levels and of different groups are in existence; and

(e) It is service oriented.

Librarianship as a Profession

Librarianship may be regarded as the one, as old as the book. But librarianship as a profession is just a little over hundred years old. Earlier it was only an occupation. The organisation of librarianship as a profession started with the establishment of the American Library Association in 1876. The imparting of specialised knowledge started with the establishment of the first library school in 1887 by Dr. Melvil Dewey. Most of the national library associations drew a set of professional ethics. During the last hundred years, it has grown rapidly and established itself as a notable profession.

The Dichotomy?

The choicest few working in special libraries, who enjoy a status at par with the executives or scientists have been trying to keep themselves away from the common core of the profession. Mr. J. Farradane in Britain started advocating since 1953 that "information work is distinct from librarianship and should in no way be confused with it." He took initiative to form the 'Institute of Information Scientists Ltd.' as distinct from The Library Association in 1958.

The *Library Association Record* of 1953 and 1954 carried a spate of letters for and mostly against the arguments of Mr. Farradane. Some described that "Farradane was thumping a rather lonely tub."

Unified View

Many librarians in UK and USA, and Dr Ranganathan and others in India were of the opinion that the difference between librarianship and information work was one of degree not kind. Information activity is rather an extension of library activity.

PROFESSION OF 'INFORMATION SPECIALISTS'

Messrs. Guinchat and Menou say that the current term for the unified profession of librarians, documentalists and information personnel, for want of a better, is 'Information Specialist.'

Work of an Information Specialist

The general type of work of all information specialists is similar. They are :

(i) Process documents and information must therefore master the technical skills involved;

(ii) Serve users and hence needs a gift for and interest in human relations; and

(iii) Need to work effectively on orderly and methodical turn of mind, a sense of organisation and imagination.

Concerns of the Information Profession

Service: An information specialist works nearly always for other people and this can occasionally be frustrating. He should continue to be useful.

Communication Skills: Personal relations of the information specialist with the users and producers of information have more decisive influence on the effectiveness of the service. Information specialist must be capable of understanding other people, mixing socially and inspiring confidence—in short, of communicating.

Judgement: There are many factors that influence information and communication. These factors change so rapidly that there is never a readymade solution or a simple rule-of-thumb for every situation. An information scientist should take decisions on taking into count of all the criteria and visualising all the implications of his judgement.

Curiosity : *The* information specialist should have curiosity to know people, organisations, things, facts, ideas and techniques so that he can make use of the right means and method for providing service.

Adaptability: The needs of the users change from time to time. So too are the knowledge and technique employed for dissemination of information. The information specialist should have an adaptive and flexible mind.

Perseverance and Modesty: Information work is always demanding; yet its immediate results are often far from impressive; besides, it is frequently the user who reaps the benefit and the praise.

CHARACTERISTICS OF THE PROFESSION

Sound Theory

Librarianship for long was based on rules-of-thumb and practices were innovated or improved on trial and error basis. Practical librarianship was by way of apprenticeship or by observation and adaptation of practices in vogue in popular and big libraries. Some of the librarians started publishing manuals and guides on several library practices for the benefit of their fellow professionals. Establishment of library associations gave opportunities for professionals to meet and discuss matters of mutual interest. Some of the leaders in the profession started bringing out basic works of guidance. The establishment of library schools gave sound and well rounded theory. Research in librarianship was initiated. Laws, rules and regulations were framed so as to assist in the day-to-day management of libraries.

Work of documentation brought-in scientists from diverse professions into the library and documentation profession. This helped the profession to understand the users better and to evolve new systems and services to meet their demands.

Information science enhanced the boundaries of the profession and disciplines. The demands of the users started changing fast. With the result there has been a great thrust on library, documentation and information professionals to understand users' needs better, understand the technology, adapt and refine them from time to time to provide pin-pointed information in an expeditious manner.

In all information units there is a natural tendency for these divisions to overlap, with the result the profession contains a large number of generalists.

Structure of the Profession

Broadly speaking there are four grades of professionals:

1. Para-professional (assistants);
2. Professional Juniors (Minimum qualification of graduation in LIS);
3. Professional Seniors—grade II (Generally postgraduates in LIS with minimum of 5 years of professional experience);
4. Professional Seniors—grade I (Managers).

Entry into the Profession

There are quite a few who enter the profession at the lower level and gradually climb up to the higher levels.

At professional junior level, the entry may be direct. They need proper orientation into the system, services and professional ethics.

At the professional senior level, the entry is by selection among experienced professionals. Their entry and their success will depend upon the maturity which they may demonstrate in their work and behaviour.

Quite sometimes, people in other professions particularly those with computer science, reprography, publishing and book trade, audio-visual media, etc., background enter the LIS profession, They undergo initial training at the appropriate level in an educational institution specialising in LIS or receive in-service training in conjunction with ad- hoc courses. Some of them may enter the profession at the fag-end of their career into library and information field. Sometimes their experience, their competence as specialists can be an asset to the organisation. But often they may not be able to cope up with the work and the demand of the profession.

Areas of Specialisation

In this profession specialist skills reflect the type of information unit; the functions of the documentary chain which it covers; and its subject fields. These criteria can, of course be combined.

The major specialisations are archival administration; library administration; information management; documentation services, etc. Particularly in the fields of information and documentation (I & D) persons with the special knowledge in the concerned discipline are preferred.

Another area of specialisation is teaching and research in LIS. Lately with the development of large information systems and networks; and the creation of complex agencies to formulate information policy, a new specialist field has emerged—the planner or manager of information. Some of the retired professionals have started offering consultancy service and liaison service.

The new occupation requires an excellent specialist background, advanced training in information science and powers of synthesis.

STATUS OF THE PROFESSION

The status of the profession is the reflection of rules which define levels of responsibility, qualifications, career prospects, duties and rewards of each position and the level of training and amount of experience required.

A few countries have established rules at the national level for a particular branch of activity or for a particular organisation. In the majority of countries, unfortunately, they are either not defined at all or only partly defined.

A recognised professional status is very important since it clarifies the relative standing of the profession and makes tt possible to attract and keep staff with requisite qualities. Without such a formal framework, there is the risk, especially for new occupations, that each individual will be dealt with in a haphazard fashion with a natural tendency to diminish

Education for the Profession

Library and Information Science (LIS) has attained due status in the universe of subjects at par with traditional disciplines. Education in library and information science is offered at various levels from school to university. At school and college level LIS is offered as an optional subject along with traditional disciplines. Special courses are also offered after school leaving certificate; post-degree programmes; as well as, postgraduate courses in LIS. Research in LIS has also picked up and several areas in the discipline are being investigated with great emphasis and vigour. Apart from the regular courses, in-service refresher courses/orientation courses into the new areas of the discipline etc., are also being organised on regular basis. New technology brought- in specialists in computer, communication, repro- and micrography and several other fields into information activity. Some of the subject specialists are also involved in processing data; information analysis, condensation, repacking, etc., providing liaison, referral and other services.

Professional Ethics

A set of moral principles and a code of conduct is a necessary guide to professional behaviour. Many of the countries have evolved written codes or ethics. Special codes were also drawn for some of the special branches of the profession. It is desirable to have a written professional code. These codes cover from general principles of dedication, devotion, determination and commitment to the profession; General social ethics of understanding the users; Social obligations of the library; Social behaviour, equality before service, etc.; Moral responsibilities of the professionals; Professional goals and objectives and means of achieving them.

The code of ethics should be prefaced with the nobility of the profession and responsibilities of the professionals.

These ethics time and again remind the professional his role, responsibilities and social commitment. The professional should keep the code of ethics before him so that they remind him the expectations of the profession. If possible a oath be administered to the new entrants in the profession to live up to the code of ethics of the profession.

Professional Organisations

Today almost all countries, regions and states have professional organisations—not one, but many. Sometimes, unhealthy competition and rivalries are also observed among the various associations. Objectives of professional associations are also different. There is a need for unified approach among various organisations. The dichotomy between library and information workers should be removed. These organisations should strive to achieve high standards in service; service to the society/nation by way of providing right information to the right user, at right time; and bring the professionals together for close association and collective thinking.

Tasks Before the Profession

Tasks in the professional work are defined by level of complexity, the general and technical knowledge required, and their related responsibilities.

There are fairly elementary routines or manipulation tasks usually performed by subordinate personnel or assistants.

Technical tasks calling for professional qualifications and in certain cases for a general one too—cataloguing, indexing, bibliographic searches, etc.

Supervision, control and organisation of the various functions of the documentary chain. These tasks require a sound professional and general training together with some experience.

Technical tasks requiring high level training and social experience in the fields or disciplines concerned, e.g.: Evaluation of information; Liaison with users, etc.

Overall design and management of the unit; teaching and research; training, internship etc.

His socio-professional standing. The danger of this is increased by the fact that the profession is too small to form a sufficiently powerful pressure group.

SOURCES USED

1. Atkinson, Frank. Librarianship: An introduction to the profession. London: Bingley, 1974, p. 7-q.
2. Guinchat, Claire and Menou, Michel. General introduction to the techniques of Information and documentation work. Paris : UNESCO. 1983. p. 329-34.
3. Kumar, P.S.G. Information science as a profession, *(in* Deshmukh. PP. *Ed.* Information systems for agricultural science and technology. New Delhi: Metropolitan, 1987. p. 184-9).
4. Kumar, P.S.G. Fundamentals of information science. Delhi: S. Chand, 1998. p. 298-305.

7

Philosophy of Librarianship*

LIBRARIANSHIP

Librarianship is in existence for thousands of years. But the emergence of librarianship as a profession in of recent origin. According to a definition "a profession is one in which its members have acquired specialised knowledge which is used either in instructing, guiding or advising others." It is obvious from the definition that librarianship is of professional nature. But, this concept is fairly recent, and it is more recent indeed, the awareness that it has certain set goals, purposes and aims. Till recently the goals are obscure and the purpose unclear. In short one failed to notice a philosophy that gives intellectual orientation and theoretical foundation behind library profession.

---

* Address at Academy of Library Science and Documentation (ALSD), Hyderabad on 22 April, 1993.

LIBRARIANSHIP AS A PROFESSION

When once librarianship is regarded as a profession and one is aware of its set goals, purposes and aims, the responsibility on the part of the librarian is doubled. He has to acquire the needed specialised knowledge and skills and abilities to achieve the set goals. It takes time to acquire the needed specialised knowledge and expert applying ability for performing the functions of an efficient librarian. In majority of situations mere application of common sense and normal intelligence will be insufficient to meet all the needs of the whole or part of the library organization. Knowledge of the aims of librarianship is needed along with the skills in applying them effectively in individual situations. Librarianship implies the development of each individual in the profession, so that he can fill successfully high position for which his abilities fit him. A librarian should have the capacity in readily responding to the needs of people he serves, A librarian in his complete and modern meaning accepts this challenge and tries to fulfil these fundamental needs.

Social and Ethical Obligation

During the past several decades great social and ethical obligations are mounting upon librarians. Librarianship, its very nature implies social ana ethical consideration. Librarianship exists for the betterment of human beings and it is indeed considered that "Better libraries and better citizens are synonymous." The modern librarianship has heartily endorsed these social and ethical obligations.

Abundant Opportunities

The field of librarianship offers abundant opportunities for the professional to acquaint with the social and ethical obligations; develop skills and abilities; and to serve his community better alongwith development of his personal stature.

With the industrial and technological revolutions, growth in economy, increase in literacy, the social pressure on libraries has increased tremendously. Librarianship offers a brilliant future for those who qualify to acquire such a position.

LIBRARIANSHIP – DEFINITION

According to Danton "Librarianship is that branch of learning which has to do with recognition, collection, organization, preservation and utilization of graphic and printed material."

Mayors defined librarianship as "That branch of human knowledge which is concerned with the production, care and use of recorded human knowledge."

From the above two definitions, we can infer that:

(i) Librarianship is a branch of human knowledge;

(ii) It is a profession;

(iii) It is a tool for information or knowledge;

(iv) It involves social service; and

(v) It is a department of scholarship, not a mere craft.

PHILOSOPHY OF LIBRARIANSHIP

Socrates stated that "Philosophy is not a search for right answer but for right question." Philosophy is the understanding of things around us and appreciation of their growth.

Philosophy of librarianship gives a broad perspective of the role, responsibilities and relationships of the librarian with that of the society in which he exists to serve. Librarian in the course of his work faces several factors about which he must take a stand. In order to deal with them, he has to develop an attitude towards them. He cannot avoid them, and as such, strike a solution best suited to the situation.

Definition

Philosophy of librarianship may be defined as a body of knowledge and beliefs that supply a broad base for determining solutions to problems of librarianship.

On problems he must timely think, quickly decide immediately put into action in managing a library. He relate judgement with objectives. He must develop good social and psychological temperament as he has to deal with readers and subordinate staff. He must have a definite, critical and evaluatory outlook about things. Develop an attitude to analyse the problems correctly and make suitable decisions For many a problem, there may not be a tailor-made solution Under these circumstances, philosophy of librarianship is useful. A librarian believes and stands for something. He cannot work in vacuum. Philosophy provides a librarian, a framework within which he can commence thinking along pathways predetermined by the philosophy.

SCHOOLS OF PHILOSOPHY OF LIBRARIANSHIP

Over the period of time various philosophical views were put forward. These are discussed below.

Practical or Actional Philosophy

Some consider librarianship as an art-pure and simple; need no theorising, thinking and rethinking. If at all there is a need for philosophy, it is practical philosophy.

The aim of librarianship is to provide service to readers.

Howley and Melvil Dewey advocated this philosophy. Dewey stressed on practical training. However, even the sense of 'know-how' needs some theoretical background.

Deductive or Organistic Philosophy

This is quite opposite to practical or actional philosophy- Here the emphasis is on the theory or theoretical study- According to this school 'practical results would be better achieved if the underlying ideas of the whole subject are clear.' The Graduate School of Librarianship, Chicago advocated this theory.

Inductive or Naturalistic or Evolutionary Philosophy

The third school advocates inductive philosophy, in the sense that conclusions are to be drawn from experience. This school emphasises on 'scientific method.' This means, collection of data (by observation or practice), drawing conclusions and fomulating principles for practical application. This needs practical experience and scientific approach. Dr. Ranganathan advocated this philosophy.

Social or Reflexive Philosophy

This school places emphasis on the relation of the library with the community. The primary function of the library is to serve the community. Butter, a protagonist of this school of thought emphasises that, "The library is a part of the society and it cannot function in isolation. Without society it has no meaning or purpose. Library as a social institution should provide an index to the ideas of the society." This philosophy is called 'social philosophy.' But, Ranganathan described this as 'reflexive philosophy.'

8

Professional Ethics*

PROFESSIONAL ETHICS

Concept

The term ethics is derived from the Greek word ethos' which means custom or character. Ethics is a set of moral principles that governs the *person*— his conduct, behaviour, character, fairness, humbleness, morality, values, commitment, duties to self improvement and to the society at large, and *his obligation*–to the profession, to the institution and the society at large.

A profession is not a profession without a set of basic or fundamental principles or ethics.

Role

Ethics helps a professional in the following ways :

1. Helps a person to know what is expected of him by the profession.
2. How he should conduct himself.

---

* Text of lecture delivered at the Acdemic Staff College, Osmania University, Hyderabad on 16 Jan 2002.

3. How he should prepare himself to meet the demands of the clientele.
4. How to uphold the values.
5. Above all to keep his profession at a higher pedestal in the eyes of the users or society in general.

LIBRARIANSHIP AND ETHICS

Ethics for Librarians

Tyler observed that "Librarianship has ethical values higher than the selfish interest of individual librarians, it expects the librarian to dedicate himself to these values and the professional group a whole, enforces discipline to see that these values are not disregarded... Librarian is primarily dedicated to the enlightement of his community, to the dissemination of truth and to the development of an enlightened citizenship." Greer has tried to explain the ethics of librarians in one word, *viz.*, loyalty, which includes loyalty to one's (i) Own work; (ii) Institutions; (iii) Fellow workers, whether in one's own or in another library; (iv) Community; and (v) Self.

Code of Ethics

According to Megnanand, there are the following aspects which should be covered in a code of ethics:

(i) Librarian and his committee;

(ii) Librarian and his staff;

(iii) Librarian and his book-suppliers;

(iv) Librarian and the book-trade;

(v) Librarian and his professional colleagues;

(vi) Librarian and his clientele;

(vii) Librarian and society; and

(viii) Librarian and the state laws and nation.

History of Professional Ethics

Professional ethics were adopted by the medical profession for the first time. Even they are expected to take an oath at the time of entering the profession. Though not spelt out as ethics, ethics of librarianship were pronounced in 1876 by Melvil Dewey in the form of motto of American Library Association, i.e., "Best Reading for the Largest Public at Least Cost." Dewey even punned on ALA as "Ask Library Anything." They were called as *'ideals'* at that time. For some time the term *"etiquette"* was used to express the concept. The term *ethics* was used for the first time by the library profession in 1908 when a discussion was arranged at Boston on the subject. The first set of ethics for librarianship was pronounced in the very next year, i.e., 1909 as "Canons of Ethics." These were revised by Mr. Botton in 1912. Mr. Botton in an article entitled, "The Ethics of Librarianship" in *The Annals of the American Academy of Political and Social Sciences* wherein he discussed the ethics of various professions in a comparative way.

The American Library Association adopted a code of ethics in 1938 prepared under the chairmanship of Ms Flora B Ledington.

Motto of Professional Ethics

We are enumerating below some ideas on the subject of professional ethics.

(i) The prime motto of professional ethics in library service is to look at the user as a patron. The service offered therefore should be done with dedication and involvement.

(ii) Being purveyor of knowledge through books and other documents, a professional has to have an abiding interest in building up his own knowledge base and should associate himself with the process of learning.

(iii) A professional has to view all creeds, dogmas and

idealisms with a professional neutrality. Personal bias, creeds, dogmas, etc., should not interfere in any way while serving a user. A library has been described as "the impartial instrument of a purposive society" (McColvin). The library should be approached with the same spirit.

(iv) A professional should uphold the sanctity of six freedoms, namely, freedom of study, freedom of thought, freedom of speech, freedom of the press, freedom of dissemination of knowledge and the freedom of instruction.

(v) The professional should voice his conviction relating to library legislation, censorship and in case when any of the above six freedoms are curbed.

The Societal Responsibility

Appreciating the value of a library as a social institution, the library staff should participate in social activities, pay attention to books and documents which support all human activities. Books and documents in fact, are corporate memories of the entire human community and therefore deserve to be preserved and protected. It is obvious, therefore, that one has to view the library as an indispensable institution for the society. The library professionals should understand this, hold a definite conviction and also make the society understand it.

User Interface

(i) Library is a storehouse of knowledge The library professional should make this knowledge accessible to all irrespective of their caste, creed or religion.

(ii) Everyone coming to the library is a learner, whether he is a renowned intellectual, a neo-literate, or a child. All of them should be given equal attention, and everyone should find the library atmosphere congenial and the library service satisfying. The library professional should establish a cordial relation with users; after all, both are seekers of knowledge.

(iii) Some persons become the readers of a library on their own. But, the library professional should try to create readers by persuasion and by publicising library activities.

Commitment to Parent Institution

The library professional should faithfully learn and execute the policies of the parent institution.

He must avoid any personal financial gain at the cost of the parent institution.

He should be fair in dealing with staff appointments, promotion etc., and while writing confidential reports of the staff working under him.

Five Laws and Professional Ethics

First Law: Books are for Use

1. While selecting books one should be unbiased. The books should be useful to the most.
2. Facilitate reading by initiating users in to the library mechanism; see that surroundings are beautiful, seating is comfortable, mechanisms are simple, rules and regulations help the users to have easy access to books.
3. Publicise the library and its services.

Second Law: Every Reader His / Her Book

1. Keep the reader at ease.
2. Adequate reference service to help the readers get the book he/she wants easily.
3. Guidance to users in the use of the library.
4. Purchase or procure a book user wants by inter-library loan.

5. Maintain union catalogues, Location lists of periodicals, etc.

Third Law: Every Book its Reader

1. The catalogue should satisfy the various approaches of the users. For this, necessary and sufficient number of added and analytical entries be provided.
2. Display new additions and less used books so that they catch the eye of the users.
3. Give good publicity of library services.
4. Organise exhibitions and extension services for popularising the library and books.

Fourth Law: Save the Time of the Reader

1. Catalogue should satisfy various approaches of the users.
2. Classification should provide easy access and easy location.
3. Provide more guides and guidance to users.
4. Introduce specialised and personalised services.

Fifth Law: Library is a Growing Organism

1. While planning library building take into consideration of future needs as well.
2. All systems should be easy to expand and even for change.
3. There should be coordination, cooperation and interaction among staff.

STAFF

Duty to Self

A professional should continually try to improve his professional knowledge and skills. One should attend in-service and refresher courses. The professional should read books, periodicals and other documents on the subject. He should enrol as a member of professional associations and participate in the conferences, seminars, etc., organised by these bodies.

It is the responsibility of the professional to protect the image of the profession. One should sacrifice petty gains and maintain high moral standards.

Duty of Colleagues

A professional should maintain cordial relation with his colleagues. Observe dignity of labour. One should sacrifice self and provide service to the staff below.

Seven Lamps of Conduct

1. *Service before self.*
2. *Unbiased.*
3. *Split-mind* (Keeping everything in mind, one should attend to all the demands of the users and colleagues simultaneously and effectively)
4. *Sympathetic behaviour* (Building confidence in users)
5. *Tact* (in dealing with users)
6. *Industry* (Putting head, hand and heart in, work)
7. Scholarship (To be a friend philosopher and guide to users, one should possess scholarship).

PROFESSIONAL ETHICS IN INDIAN CONTEXT

Professional forums should be free of personal philosophies, attitudes, and prejudices as well as vested interests of individuals. The professional societies have a great influence on professional development. Active collaboration and participation of members are necessary to have a strong and effective professional body. The library and information personnel should take pride in professional ethos, activities and service. Nothing should be done to denigrate our profession, especially in outside forums. The senior professionals should encourage younger generation and be a source of emulation by their exemplary service. The professionals should cultivate their field of knowledge and enrich it by research, teaching and dissemination through literature. There should be excellent cooperation among professionals in order to foster resource sharing, interlibrary loan, networking of libraries, etc.

The library and information personnel should be very particular about personal ethics. They should avoid unlawful and unethical pecuniary interests. Book purchase and other financial transactions in libraries are vulnerable issues for abuse. The professionals should exercise abundant caution. Their integrity should be beyond doubt in such matters. With colleagues, patrons and management, their dealings should be fair and just and relations most cordial and friendly.

The ethics of the profession has been a subject matter of discussion in professional forums for a long time. In 1989 the Joint Council of Library Associations in India (JOCLAI) had finalised a draft code of ethics. It is now under circulation for eliciting comments and suggestions. Thereafter, it is expected to be formally adopted on behalf of the profession. It is this welcome step which prompted me to write this editorial at this juncture with an appeal to the professional community to consider the code of ethics as very sacred to be followed in letter and spirit. Let our commitment to observe the code of ethics in practice be firm and strong. At no other time than now, the code of ethics for library and information professionals is necessary. The code that is being adopted should be made known widely among the professionals. The schools of library and information science should familiarise their students, who are the future professionals, with the contents and significance of the code. So also, all the library and information science associations and societies should circulate the code to all their members and obtain their solemn undertaking/assurance of their observance of the code while discharging their duties and responsibilities.

Code of Ethics adopted by JOCLAI

Preamble

We the librarians and information professionals of India, convinced of the fact that a library is meant to fulfil certain definite educational, cultural and socio-economic objectives of the contemporary society;

Realising that we have a clearly defined effective role to play in the fulfilment of these objectives;

Aware of the fact that this role, modified from time to time with the introduction of new innovations in information techniques and the overall development of our technological society, will continue in the foreseeable future;

Believing that in our democratic society, following a socialistic pattern, every citizen has the right to intellectual freedom and the freedom of access to undistorted, unbiased information, irrespective of his educational, cultural level, political affiliation, caste, creed, religion, age or sex and that we are committed to foster readers rights to read as they please, except such material which are covered by censorship regulations imposed by law;

Accepting our special responsibility of selecting reading materials and guiding lay public in their use of the library's resources, to enlarge their mental horizon and elevate their taste.

Considering that we are not simply a congregation of certain related groups of technicians and managers, but a homogeneous group of educators, equipped with general education and proper training in modern techniques and technology of library management, continuously updated to keep pace with the changing needs of our progressive society;

Conscious fully of the fact that membership in our profession carries with it special obligations to maintain the highest level of personal integrity and competencies, and;

Determined to create a healthy professional tradition for the future; create and give upto ourselves the following code of professional ethics:

The Code

1. Library and information profession is a service profession. Library and information professionals should gather information, organise into easily accessible collections, provide mechanisms that help productive utilisation of the same by all the eligible clientele.
2. Library and information professionals must be governed by the democratic principle of giving every user his/her opportunity to access to information resources and make special efforts to keep their interests growing towards further developments.
3. Library and information professionals must familiarise themselves with all available information sources that are of interests of their clientele either on demand or in anticipation. They may be in the form of books, technical papers, and other non-print records and even sometimes specialist in any field of knowledge. Gathering, organising and transmitting information to the appropriate targets of use is an essential credo of librarians and information personnel efficiency and effectiveness in finding targets of use for every information available is the main focus of our profession.
4. Library and information professionals must keep service orientation in their professional work. Person] philosophies and attitudes should not interfere with those of the institutional organisations.
5. Library and information professionals should avoid unlawful and unethical pecuniary interests and must serve their clientele on an equitable basis.

6. Library and information professionals should keep timeliness as a prime factor in serving information to user. A delayed response brings discredit to the service and ultimately may not be useful.
7. Library and information professionals should aim at the development of their own professional organisations and take pride in the ethos, activities and services. They should encourage younger generation of professionals with their own exemplary service.
8. Library and information professionals should cultivate their field of knowledge in a professional way. They should contribute to the field by the research, teaching and dissemination through literature.

SOURCES USED

1. Chatterjee (Amitabha). Ethics of librarianship: A Literature survey. *[IASLIC Bull,* v 10; 1965. pp. 143-5).
2. Dr. B.R, Ambedkar Open University, (Hyderabad). Professional Ethics. {Course Material), pp, 15-6.
3. *ILA Bulletin,* Editorial (v. 24; 1989. pp 175-7).
4. Mittal (R.L.) Ethics of librarianship. (*in* Author's Library Administration. Chap 3. pp. 24-32).

TECHNOLOGY

9

Changing Role of Libraries in the Technological Environment*

TECHNOLOGY AND LIBRARIES

In the opinion of Bhattacharya "There are certain activities traditionally associated with libraries - such as, acquisition, serial control cataloguing and circulation. Today the term 'Library Automation' is used extensively to refer primarily to the use of computers to perform some of the traditional library activities such as those mentioned above. Conventionally, some related fields such as, information retrieval, automatic indexing and abstracting, automatic textual analysis, etc. do not generally fall within the purview

* Keynote Address delivered at the "State Level Conference on Role of College Librarian in the Information Network Era" organised by VMV.Com JNT Arts and JJP Science College, Nagpur on 6 Sep. 2010.

of 'Library Automation'. But this distinction is generally disappearing; for example, 'information retrieval' is now included within its purview, so also, is the case with net working. Though computers play the primary roles in library automation today, yet the roles played by telecommunication technology and the reprography technology are of great significance because of the extent of support they offer to library automation." This study, though mainly aims to survey the automation of traditional library activities, it also deals with computerzation of inforrnation work, with an overview of the telecommunication and reprography technologies in India.

ADVANTAGES OF AUTOMATION

Automation has the following advantages :

1. Large data can be handled with ease and accuracy
2. Operates at a great speed and promptness
3. High rate and better quality in performance
4. Labour saving
5. Cost effective
6. Ease in functioning
7. Avoids/eliminates duplication of work
8. Greater manipulation possible

AREAS OF AUTOMATION

Areas of automation in libraries can be categorised into two:

1. House - keeping and
2. Information handling

HOUSE KEEPING OPERATIONS

1. Acquistion
2. Classification

3. Cataloguing
4. Indexes and Thesauri
5. circulation
6. Stock-taking
7. Serial Control

INFORMATION HANDLING

1. Current Awareness Services
2. Selective Dissmination of Information
3. Retrospective Search Systems.

BASICS OF COMPUTERZATION

1. Variety of media

Library is a growing organism. Collection grows. But staff position does not improve proportionately.

For instance - in the library area - reference books may be available only in CD-ROMS. Catalog publications may be available only on floppies or similar medium. Journals may be available in electronic form etc.

2. System Analysis (Requirements Specification)

This stage of investigation answers the question "what must be achieved through computerisation"?

This is done by thorough investigation of all departments of the library, various procedures, forms / registers, persons involved, flow of information, flow of work *etc.* Objectives as to what must be done are agreed upon with people concerned in specific terms. For example -" We should be able to send reminders for unsupplied books at least four times a year to every vendor".

Objectives : Formulation can be economic, technical, or social. "It should cut down cost of ordering activity by 50%."

"All programming will be done in DBASE II" (as we do not wish to recruit specialists for the task). No retrenchment may be allowed as a result of computerisation etc.

3. System Design

Here we try to answer - "How do we achieve the objectives stated in detail in step 2?"

Stages 1 and 2 are leg work and this design stage is brain work.

This is the most highly technical area where the System Analyst develops several models and decides on the best among the various alternative approaches to tackle the problem. He keeps in mind the organisational constraints and user's requirements and balances judiciously.

How exactly data will be generated, validated, stored and made available for processing by the computer etc. are decided in this stage.

4. Development

Carrying out what has been decided in the 'Design' stage earlier, is development. In the case of Library Acquisition computersation for example, this will involve writing of the program code, entering it into the computer, compiling, editing etc.

This job is the responsibility mainly that of the applications programmer.

In this stage, which may be longest if the programs are developed inhouse, may call for a great deal of finer details.

Buying a ready made software package reduces this stage to a shortone. It is only needed to install, get trained in inputing data and start using the system.

5. Testing

Once the program are written and checked out for

syntax errors, it is tested.

The programmer answers the question:

"Will this program ever work?" in the first phase of testing. Then he obtains sample data as well as manually arrived at results (output) from the user. The samples provided should be such that all the facilities provided in the program must be tested. For instance if Library Acquisition provides for checking automatically if the invoice amount is more than the price in the order by 15%, the data in sample bill given for testing should contain at least one bill for this aspect of testing, the results you get and the results you ought to get are compared. User involvement is high in this stage.

Programs are corrected and process repeated until it is totally error free.

6. Implementation

Implementation of computer based systems may be of three types : a) Parallel Running, b) Pilot Running, c) Overnight change.

(a) Parallel Running : In this method both manual method and computer processing are done simultaneously. Manual method is relied upon for day to day working. Results of computer processing are constantly compared and checked for discrepancies.

It should be borne in mind that errors could be due in existing manual process also! (This may come to light due to high level of accuracy of computerisation). This method is time consuming and the period needed for wholesale with over can't be easily predicted. Moreover additional temporary hands are needed for checking errors. But this provides a safe method.

For instance in the case of a book ordering activity, parallel running may be worthwhile as errors in wrong ordering may be expensive.

(b) Pilot Running : In this method two situations are possible. In one case, among the whole target user group, a small section is identified and they are served by computer system. Rest are served by manual system. This is called Pilot Running. All aspects of provisions of the software are tried on the small group of select users.

Alternately, a specified module of the program package may be implemented initially. After gaining confidence, computerisation may be extended using other modules. This is called Phased Implementation.

For example if you have developed a circulation system, you may try it out initially with all staff members who are more likely to respond with responsibility , tolerate errors, offer feedback etc. (than student population).

Again, if you have obtained a software package for all functions of the library activities, you may just wish to implement one of them - Say, Acquisition Control - to begin with.

(c) Overnight Change : Obviously this means - set a date and start the new system from then on - No manual system is available as parallel or back up facility. Though risks are high, in this method of implementation, there is no money wasted in terms of time, error checking etc. As all persons will be in the same boat, rectification of errors will be speedy.

If you are starting a new service afresh or which is substantially different from earlier service (say SDI), you can straight away opt for this method.

However each organisation has to weigh the advantages and disadvantages of the above three methods and perhaps use them in combinations as well.

7. Running

When the system is up and running there is no much to do except keep - up schedules. You may have to provide for emergencies such as staff on vacation, or sudden leave; power shut downs, computer down time, etc.

8. Review

A fairly running system needs to be reviewed periodically. Reviews will reveal whether we are within the budgets allotted; and whether time frames are being adhered to or not. They may even tell us whether the objectives with which computerisation was started have been achieved or not. Results of Review stage will help as input for further computerisation work.

LIBRARY STAFF INVOLVEMENT IN COMPUTERISATION

Right from stage 1 to stage 8 mentioned above the concerned library staff should be actively involved.

In the initial study, it is librarian who identifies repetitive jobs, jobs involving delay etc. In. the second stage - specialization of requirements or system analysis - most active involvement is envisaged. Every activity must be observed and explained. Present procedures must be demonstrated and explained. Deviations or exceptions should be spelt out. Librarian must prepare his staff for change. This involves coaxing, understanding, removing fears, regarding etc.

Librarian must be involved in Data Validation / error checking stages during design stages. He should also clarify which jobs will be manual and which ones will be computer handled.

The design shown by System Analyst Should be fully understood by the Librarian. Librarian should review the contents of the various reports presented during the above stage with respect to:

(a) Terms of reference

(b) Scope of the Stage

(c) Recommendations
(d) Plans and time scales
(e) Costs and budgets
(f) Manpower needed etc.

During the program development stage Librarian can get his staff trained for operation, data entry etc. he can also plan develop manual procedures to 'fall back' if needed.

During testing stage, Librarian should give valid test data. He should monitor the progress of development in each stage.

New clerical data preparation procedures if any should be explained to staff.

PROGRAM PACKAGES

Three Types of Software

Software or the programs that make computers do what we want or needed. They can be grouped under three broad categories: 1) System Software 2) General Purpose Software, 3) Specific Application Packages.

System Software

Under the first category we may include such things like Operating Systems, Compilers, Translations, Interpreters, Debuggers, Utilities or Tool kits for enhancing the use of the computer as a whole etc.

General Purpose Software

General purpose software may perhaps consist of Word Processing Software, Spread Sheet packages, DBMS packages etc. Some popular Word Processing Software are : WORDSTAR WORDLORD, WORDPERFECT, etc., VISICALC, SUPERCALC, LOTUS 123, are spread sheets. Important and popular DBMS packages are dBASE II, dBASE III, dBASE III PLUS, KNOWLEDGEMAN, FOXBASE, RBASE etc.

Application Software

We are primarily interested now in the third category: Specific application packages that are of interest to Librarians.

In a Library the following and similar other major functions may be computerised:

1. Acquistions Control
2. Serials Control
3. Circulation Control
4. Information Retrieval
5. Selective Dissemination of Information
6. Publishing Abstracting Bulletins
7. List of Additions
8. Current Awareness Bulletin.

Total or Piece-meal

We can get total integrated Software Package capable of taking care of most of the functions mentioned above. Or we may buy specific application package say for acquisition control alone.

Bought or Made at home

Again the application package may be developed within the library or bought from outside. It can also be developed, exclusively for us, by an outside consultancy based upon the detailed specification given by us.

Networks

LANs, WANs, and Network Connections

The two basic types of network are Local Area Networks (LANs) and Wide Area Netwoks (WANs). A LAN links computers that are physically close to each other and usually 'hard wired' together via cables. Typically, LANs are used in single organizations at single sites. WANs, however, can cover large distances, within and beyond national boundaries.

Internet Technology

Among all networking technologies, the internet technology is most useful and economically vaible in the era of present communication system. The term "Internet" comes from a concept called inter-networking that denotes interaction between networks of computers. It is a vast collection of large and small inter-connected networks extending all the way across the world. The Internet World Wide Web (WWW.w3 or web) is, therefore, a vast electronic library made-up of millions of pages of information stored in hundreds of thousands of linked computers around the globe. It is basically a network of computers in the world providing major information services. Thus, Information Super Highway enable the following:

- User from any part of the world can connect or access information irrespective of time and space factors.
- Users on this worldwide network can exchange electronic mail with one another within a few seconds.
- User can talk with one another online.

Internet is thus, an international network of networks. More than 30,000 network are connected among 71 countries through internet. In each of these countries there is atleast one backbone computer which operates at a very high speed to carry the bulk of traffic load. In India VSNL's Gateway Internet Access Services (GIAS) Network of VSNL is working as the backbone for other networks. India has its main internet access node at USA via satellite media and to internet node in Europe via sub-marine cable media.

To give a few examples, the Internet can be used to:

- exchange personal messages with colleagues, friends or relatives at other network sites, information and ideas with people who share a common interest and seek information from them.

- automatically receive information on world events, leisure interests and technical, business and professional matters by subscribing to electronic journals, conferences, newsletters and alerting services.
- look up information in reference works, databases and libraries worldwide.
- retrieve journal articles, books, computer programs and graphic images and transfer them to a personal computer.
- make use of computer facilities that are not available locally.
- download new software or updates for existing applications.
- browse catalogues of goods and services and make credit - card purchases.
- participate in distance learning and academic conferencing.
- engage in real-time 'chat' and multi-player interactive games.
- communicate with individuals or groups by means of voice only or voice and image
- publish information for access by other Internet users.

OPAC

Online Public Access Catalog (OPAC)

Computerized cataloguing has finally produced Online Public Access Catalogue (OPAC). but it must be emphasized that not all online catalogues are public catalogues. An often encountered combination for instance, has been an online access facility for library staff and an offline, e.g. microfiche, catalogue for the user. However OPAC has overshadows all other events in the history of cataloguing during the past decade. OPAC can be accessed via a computer terminal. Such catalogues allow any members of the community to search the catalogue data base in order to see if the library holds specific title of document, to be informed of its location in the library and if the catalogue system is linked to the circulation system, the enquirer be intimated whether the item is readily available or is on loan to other etc.

Bibliographical Databases

Bibliographical database contains descriptive information about documents - books, periodical articles- the data typically included in these databases are titles, authors, journal names, volume and number, dates, keyboards, abstracts, etc. Inquiries about the database are intended to develop a list of document numbers or references which satisfy the needs of users concerning a particular subject, such databases exist for numerous fields.

Categories of bibliographic Databases

Exchange of information through electronic mail, online facility or a terminal is possible if a database is created. A database is an organised, integrated and often inter-related collection of computer-based data, records, files, or information. According to John Convey databases are collections of records in machine-readable form that are made available for searching from remote computer terminals. In bibliographic databases the data stored comprises inputs of bibliographic details of a document for identification storage and retrieval purposes. Bibliographic database can be divided into two categories:

1. Internal databases and associated services:
2. External databases and associated services.

The internal bibliographic databases are those created by libraries and information centres of their published holding such as:

1. books

2. serials
3. articles in periodicals
4. proceedings of conferences, subject reports etc.
5. manuscripts, theses, etc.

External bibliographic databases comprise online catalogues of the following types:

1. Abstracting and citation databases like PSYCINFO, the machine readable counterpart of *Psychological abstracts*. And SCISERCH, the machine readable counterpart of Science Citation Index and Current Contents, the publications of the Institute for Scientific Information, USA.
2. Local, metropolitan, regional, national and international bibliographic networks. The following are examples.

   Local : A network in a camps or an institution such as IIT Bombay or IIT Kanpur.

   Metropolitan : A city network like DELNET or CALIBNET.

   Regional : A proposed network like NELIBNET for North-East India

   National : A network like INFLIBNET.

   International : A network like OCLC that has outgrown its local, regional and national character and is used the world over.
3. Databases of indexes to newspaper e.g. *New York Times Information Index* or *National Newspapers Index* published in USA.
4. Databases of of union catalogues e.g. *National Union Catalogue of Scientific Serials in India* (INSDOC)

5. Databases of references sources like *Ulirch's Periodical Directory*.
6. Full text databases provide the relevant information directly and give complete texts of documents. *Harvard Business Review* (HBR) offers both bibliographic and text details.

Many of the world databases are now made accessible to the users by vendors - computer - based agencies that arrange access to various world databases for a fee. For instance vendors like DIALOG, SDC and Data - Star offer INSPEC database to users as well as access to similar databases. For instance DIALOG Information Services Inc, Palo Alto, California offers access to more than 400 databases.

Data Banks

Files containing data on entities in the same category are brought together and integrated into one files and made available to a wide variety of users. This is called a 'Data Bank', to use the analogy of a bank, the user can deposit or withdraw from several branches.

Multimedia

Multimedia is a combination of some or all forms such as text, data images, photographs, animation$_s$ audio and video, which are converted from different formats into a uniformat digital media and is delivered by computers. Unlike the analogue media, the digital media which allows users to manipulate according to the needs. Use at their pace and interact at any point of the program when a multimedia program is developed in a hypertext environment, the resulting product is called 'hypermedia' so multimedia wold then be a part of the hypermedia products but not vice-versa. The basic difference between these two is in the organization and linkage of the information fragments.. The information fragments in multimedia are organized linearly non-linearly organized with links to' each other.

The main elements of the multimedia are:

1. **Text :** Information about an object or event etc.

   Notes, captions, subtitles, contents, indexes, dictionaries and help facilities.

2. **Data :** Tables, charts, graphs, spreadsheets, statistics and raw data.

3. **Graphics :** Both traditional and computer generated such as drawing, points, maps etc.

4. **Photographic images :** Negatives, slides, prints, video cameras etc.

5. **Animation :** Including both computer generated, video etc.

6. **Audio :** It includes speech and music digitised form cassettes, tapes, CDs etc.

7. **Video :** Either converted from analogue film of entirely created within a computer.

Impact of Multimedia

Multimedia, not only helps the users in providing information from different media on one platform, but also gave on space, money, maintenance, operational convergences etc. The major advantages of multimedia in libraries are:

(a) It can help satisfying different information needs such reference, enrichment, entertainment, leisure etc.

(b) It can help meeting various types of information preference of the users such as scholarly, scientific, vocational, artistic, recreational etc.

(c) Being a digital format, information can also be accessed by remote users on a network. It also helps in overcoming the accommodated users.

(d) It is interesting and easy to use over the existing form such as print, microforms, online etc.

(e) Its control and interactivity helps the users and provides the benefits of books and human beings.

Digital Libraries

Digital library is a relatively new concept. The term digital library explains the nature of its collection. Many definitions are available in the literature. Digital libraries are electronic libraries in which large number of geographically distributed users and diverse repositories of electronic objects. Electronic objects include networked text, images, maps, sounds, videos, catalogues of merchandise and scientific, business and government dataset. They also include hypertext, hypermedia and multimedia compositions (Yerkey, 1996). A vivid account of what a digital library means, technologies involved and the intellectual property in the cyberspace have been provided by Lyman (1996). another work useful for those who plan digital libraries is by Saffady (1995) published under Library Technology Reports.

A digital library is understood to have the information stored predominantly in electronic or digital medium. The digital information collections may include digital books, digital/scanned images, graphic, textual and numeric data, digitised films, audio and video clips etc. A digital library is expected to provide access to the digital information collections.

Challenges, Issues and Concerns

A number of challenges are to be faced before digital libraries could be planned, established and functioned well. Crawford (1998) provides some food for thought as to when a library should convert into a digital library:

(a) When reading form digital devices is as comfortable, effective and fast as reading from printed books and serials (or more so) and

(b) When digital reading and storage devices are omnipresent, and

(c) When digital distribution replaces print publishing for all new materials because it is cheaper, faster, and better and

(d) When all existing library materials are converted to digital form and

(e) When digital communication facilities are so fast inexpensive that transmission of publication equivalent is essentially instantaneous and free and

(f) Given that publishers would not stand in the way of institutions making single purchased or converted publications simultaneously available throughout the institution, nation or world, then : (only) libraries will and must convert to digital distribution as a more effective way to carry out their missions.

ELECTRONIC JOURNALS

Electronic Journals - Indian Scenario

In India, many research libraries and some university libraries are already accessing the electronic counterpart of the printed journals, which they are subscribing to. Most of these journals have the online access free along with the print subscription. For the last two or three years, many publishers and vendors were experimenting with their different pricing strategies to the libraries in India. Some of them started the offer of online access to the electronic journals free on a trial basis, wherever the libraries were subscribing to their print versions. As a next step, a few publishers offered their electronic journals for a nominal fee in addition to the print journals. The publishers were trying to arrive at a price, suitable to the libraries, especially for those in the developing countries (Louis, et al.2001).

While the libraries in North America and Europe were accessing the online journals, the libraries in India were still struggling to set up the infrastructure required for online access to journals. As a result, there is a delay in acquiring the electronic journals and databases in Indian libraries. Additionally, our library budgets do not give the flexibility to buy the much-required high- tech format of the information . Librarians are in a fix, as to how to manage accessing information within their budget. In addition, they are also expected to bargain for accessing more information. This is precisely what libraries in other countries have managed by establishing some formal networks like consortia, which have the ability to bargain collectively with the commercial, publishers. The same concept or the trend has spread to our country in recent times. More and more publishers have shown interest and willingness to have a dialog with librarians in India. They expect the librarians to have a formal commitment among themselves before they start bargaining with the publishers. In the absence of standardized formal consortia arrangements within the country, it is a difficult situation for Indian libraries to accept the existing procedure for consortia models in other-countries.

The objective of this study is to establish some guidelines for the formation of consortia among Indian libraries, especially to administer the electronic journals in Science and Technology disciplines.

ACCESS

Consortia Approach

Consortia are nothing but cooperative effort, which manages all the library services collectively. It has the purpose of exploring the need for libraries to make the most effectiveness of their funds collectively. This partnership fosters pride, determination and as sense of ownership between its a constituent libraries and staff. Consortia are regarded as an effective strategy to increase the buying power of individual libraries over the short term and as an opportunity to maximize the efforts of cooperative collection building for resource sharing over the long term (Richer, 1999). It is essential to understand the definition of the term "consortium" which is a powerful cooperative strategy.

The following definitions from the available sources are the derivation from the basic term of "consortium".

A consortium is said to be "a cooperative arrangement among groups or institutions, or an association or society" (American Heritage Dictionary)

The need for an Indian national consortium of libraries to share the access to, and cost of the electronic journals has often been discussed in many forums. Since there is no common base for many of the libraries, which would benefit from the consortium membership, the concept of a widely agreed consortium has not materialized in India so far. The few consortia, which have sprung up in the last two years, have managed to take off and also sustain until now, due to different reasons.

Free Open Source Software (FOSS)

'Briefly, OSS/FS programs are programs whose licenses give users the freedom to run the program for any purpose, to study and modify the program, and to redistribute copies of either the original or modified program (without having to pay royalties to previous developers). — *David Wheeler*

Free and Open Source Software (FOSS) has become an international phenomenon, moving from relative obscurity to being the latest buzzword in a few short years. However, there is still a lack of understanding about what really constitutes FOSS and the ramifications of this new concept. To better explain this phenomenon, we will examine the philosophy and development methods being FOSS.

The FOSS Philosophy

There are two major philosophies in the FOSS world : the Free Software Foundation (FSF) philosophy and the Open Source Initiative (OSI) Philosophy. We begin with the FSF philosophy, due to its historical precedence.

According to the FSF, free software is about protecting four user freedoms:

- The freedom to run a program, for any purpose:
- The freedom to study how a program works and adapt it to a person's needs. Access to the source code is a precondition for this;
- The freedom to redistribute copies so that you can help your neighbour and
- The freedom to improve a program and release your improvements to the public, so that the whole community benefits. Access to the source code is a precondition for this.

At the heart of FSF is the freedom to cooperate. Because non-free (Free as in freedom, not price) software restricts the freedom to cooperate, FSF, considers non-free software unethical. FSF is also opposed to software patents and additional restrictions to existing copyright laws. All of these restrict the four user freedoms listed above. For a more detailed explanation of why software needs to be free, please refer to the FSF explanation,"Why software should be Free", found at http://www.fsf.org/philosophy/shoudbefree.html

The OSI Philosophy is Somewhat Different

The basic idea behind open source is very simple: When programmers can read, redistribute and modify the source code for a piece of software, the software evolves. People improve it, people adapt it, people fix bugs. And this can happen at a speed that, if one is used to the slow pace of conventional software development, seems astonishing.

The OSI is focused on the technical values of making powerful, reliable software and is more business-friendly than the FSF. It is less focused on the moral issues of Free Software and more on the practical advantage of the FOSS distributed development method.

Role of College Libraries

Interestingly technology brought the world close, it has reduced the distance, increased the growth and removed the divide. Every one can have access to the new development. College libraries in their own humble way adopt the new technology and improve the access to the world of information.

Events of this nature will inspire the college librarians to initiate computerisation, improve the services and increase the use by the users.

10

Indian Response to International Developments in ICT*

EMERGENCE OF COMPUTERS

First Generation

Charles Babbage first conceived of the Difference Engine and Analytical Engine in the early nineteenth century, as automatic devices to perform a sequence of operations. He could not have visualized the phenomenal developments that were to take place in the following century and a half. In fact, Babbage did not even succeed in completing his machine. It was only in 1944 that the Mark-I designed by Howard Aiken was built at Harvard University. This Automatic Sequence Controlled Calculator is widely regarded as the first computer. This was a mechanical

* Keynote Address delivered at State Level Seminar on "Librarian and ICT" at Shri Sant Gajanan Maharaj Engineering College, Shegaon, on 16 Feb. 2008.

machine unlike the electronic machine of today. Earlier to this, in Germany Konard Zuse is known to have developed the Zuse Z3 computer in 1941. But, little is known about this machine.

Second Generation

The first truly electronic computer was the Electronic Numerical integrator and Computer (ENIAC) designed by Mauchly and Eckert and completed at the University of Pennsylvania in 1946-47. ENIAC employed electronic components unlike the electro-mechanical components used by Mark-I, UNIVAC-1 by the same designers, became in 1951, the first commercially available large computer. Unlike encoded paper tapes used in Mark-I, in ENIAC operations were specified by connecting a groups of wires. But connecting wires and cables for small non-repetitives tasks was too high to be practical.

EARLY APPLICATION IN LIBRARIES

Indexing

Dissatisfaction with the pre-coordinated indexes have led people to devise post-coordinate systems which eliminate pre-ordering of the concepts, etc. In a post-coordinate

Important post-coordinate systems are :

(i) Mortimer Taube's Uniterm system,

(ii) Calvin Mooers Zator System,

(iii) Cordonnier's Selecto System.

Title Based Keyword Indexes

The use of computers in the field of index has increased with the pioneering work of Luhn of IBM on the KWIC (Key Word In Context) index. Since then a number of variations of KWIC index like KWOC (Key Word Out of Context), KWAC (Key Word Away from Context), etc. have emerged.

Unit Record Systems

A large number of book catalogues were produced in the US in the 1940s using unit record machines. In a unit record system, the cataloguing information is keypunched and the punched cards are then sorted into a desired filing sequence using the sorters. Sorted cards are then processed using the tabulators to obtain either book catalogues or card catalogues.

Computer Based Systems

MARC Project

The introduction of computers in the late 1950s accelerated the use of automated techniques in the Library of Congress (LC). The appointment of King Committee to survey the Mechanization in Information Retrieval (IR) in 1958 can be regarded as a corner-stone in the progress towards automation at the LC. The final report of this survey funded by the Council for Library Resources (CLR) was published in 1963. This report envisaged the possibility of automating the entire bibliographic system of the LC within ten years. Encouraged by this report the CLR awarded a contract to LC for converting its catalogue to a machine readable form for the purpose of printing bibliographical products by computers. For this LC acquired two big computers, an IBM 1401 with four tape units and an IBM 1403 in 1963. This study was reported at a conference held in LC in January 1965. In December 1965, LC received a further grant from CLR for the development of a pilot operation to test the feasibility and utility of the distribution of machine readable catalogue data to user libraries. This project was called 'MARC'.

COMPUTERS IN INDIA

Contribution of ancient India to computer technology

Aryabhatta, the ancient Indian mathematician, had no

computer but some of the techniques which he developed are precisely the ones used in solving problems with today's computers.

There is an amazing similarity in the codes of artificial intelligence machines and the way the ancient grammarians of India paraphrased the Sanskrit language.

According to Subash Kak, Professor Electrical and Computer Engineering in the Lousian State University in the United States, computer designers in the west are now studying the works of Indian mathematicians to get a tip or two about writing software.

Aryabhatta's 'Algorithm' called Kuttaka, meant to solve linear intermediate equations, was found to be "extremely efficient computationally", Kak said.

Similarly, the method of Brahmagupta, Jayadeva and Bhaskara II- which was rediscovered in Europe 1000 years later - was "optimum in minimising the number of steps" for solving a problem.

Kak mentioned that a comprehensive analysis of the contributions of Indian grammarians had recently been made by an American computer engineer, Dr Rick Briggs.

In a paper published in the 1985 issue of *Artificial Intelligence*, Dr. Briggs said that ancient Indians developed a method for paraphrasing Sanskrit "in a manner that is identical not only in essence but also in form with current work of artificial intelligence."

According to Dr. Briggs, "Sanskrit grammarians have already found a way of solving what is perhaps the most important problem in computer science natural language understanding and machine translation."

Growth

The first computer system to come to India was the HEC-II computer brought by the Indian Statistical Institute in 1956. Esso was the first firm in India to use a computer for commercial purposes. This was in the year 1961. Computers started appearing in a big way on the Indian scene in the mid-1960s. The Indian Institute of Technology, Kanpur and the Tata Institute of Fundamental Research, Bombay established computer centres in 1963-64. By 1970 there were about 120 computers installed in about 106 organizations scattered in 24 towns all over India. The number had gone upto 300 by 1975; and to over 600 by 1980. In 1982 alone, it was estimated, about 750 computers were to be installed in India. PCs have changed the scene totally in 1970s.

COMMUNICATION TECHNOLOGY IN INDIA

"In ancient times those who controlled the roads and caravan routes held the power. In the fifteenth through the nineteenth centuries, control of the seas was a basis for power. In the twenty-first century whoever control the international electronic networks will surely wield the power." says Williams. Such is the potentiality of communication technology.

The New Era of Satellite Communication

1965 heralded a new era in communication with the orbitting of 'Early Bird' telecommunication satellite by the United States. India started taking advantage of INTELSAT on completion of the ground station in 1974 at Pune.

By 1980 India had 24,77,000 telephone and 7600 telephone exchanges. There were 3,20,000 km wire lines, and 18,000 under-ground co-axial cables. Rs. 60 crore were allocated to telecommunications in the First Five-Year Plan. In the Sixth Five-Year Plan, it was increased to 3000 crores.

Satellite Communication in India

India has developed sufficient technological capabilities to plan, design, build and test satellites for scientific experiments.

India has made substantial progress in launching

technology also. The first experimental Satellite Launch Vehicle SLV-3 (E)-01 was launched in 1979. The SLV-3 (E)-02 was fired into space successfully in 1980. A more advanced version of SLV-3 called ASLV (Augmented Satellite Launch Vehicle) which can launch a satellite of 150 kg has been designed and review has been completed. India has achieved success in launching a 600 kg class satellite with PSLV (Polar Satellite Launch Vehicle).

The INSAT Scheme

The INSAT-1 (Indian National Satellite-1) system is a multipurpose operational geostationary satellite system combining mainly three major subsystems, namely telecommunications, nationwide TV broadcasting, and meterol-ogical capacity. Unfortunately, the INSAT-1A system launched in 1982 had a premature end. However, INSAT-1B launched in 1983 is a success and it is being fully exploited for all the three major functions that are envisaged. The P & T Department has established thirty one earth stations for providing nationwide network.

INFORMATION SYSTEMS AND NETWORKS

International Information Systems

There has been rapid development of information systems and programs. Most of these are international in many respects. Those which are international in scope and coverage of materials were called international systems earlier. An information system or a bibliographical project is now international in many more respects. In fact, the national or international or universal has changed. In any system, now, there is a considerable amount of decentralization of efforts and activities. The input data created at different national focal points are merged and processed at the international centre and the processed data are sent back to national focal points for providing services to their immediate users.

Redesigning of National Services

National input ensures for each participating country, the receipt of a complete data base generated by the international agency. The usefulness of such a data base depends on the national services that can be planned and provided from them. The two most important services that are usually thought of in this context are SDI and bibliographical services - both on demand and in anticipation.

PARTICIPATION IN INTERNATIONAL SYSTEMS

Bhabha Atomic Research Centre

International Nuclear Information System Data Base: The International Nuclear Information System (INIS) is a computer based information system providing bibliographic description and abstracts of documents published in the field of nuclear science and technology. It is sponsored by International Atomic Energy Agency (IAEA), Vienna and started functioning in April 1970. The INIS Atomindex was started in May 1970. This is a semi-monthly and it covers the world's output in nuclear science and technology literature. As a by-product of this indexing and abstracting service, the magnetic tapes containing the INIS *Atomindex* are made available to the participating member states. These tapes containing machine readable files constitute the INIS data base. The INIS system is an example of an international data base with decentralized input and centralized output.

The Library and Information Services (L & IS) of the BARC, Bombay is the national input centre for INIS and receives the INIS output on magnetic tapes. The tapes are received by airmail every month and each tape contains two Atomindex issues. The INIS output tapes are half an inch in width and available as seven tracks with a density of 556 cpi or nine track with densities 800, 1600, or 2400 cpi. The INIS data base can be used for

A. Literature search,

B. SDI, and

C. Compilation of bibliographies.

The INIS-IRMS (Information Retrieval Management System) software package can be used for providing various information services. The processing of INIS data base at the L & IS, BARC was planned in two stages :

A. Providing SDI service.

B. Providing retrospective literature search.

SDI Service : The user is requested to give his subject interest in narrative form, underlining the terms which he thinks are important. The concepts are then identified and indexed using the INIS treasures. Using the index term-descriptors, a query is prepared. The set of cards punched accordingly is the user profile. This is run against the inverted file of descriptors using a computer program to find the document numbers which answers the final query positively. The extracted documents are sorted in ascending order using the fixed record length file, the bibliographic details of the documents in suitable format are printed. The abstracts are also included. The query cards and the number of documents retrieved are also printed. The user is requested to give a feedback on the print-out supplied to him. The user profile is updated on the basis of the feedback.

The retrospective search service could not be taken up immediately because of the additional storage capacity required and different set of computer programs needed for file updating and maintenance.

Indian Council of Agricultural Research

AGRIS Programme : The Sixteenth Congress of FAO held in November 1971 adopted a resolution endorsing the AGRIS Programme and asked the Director General of FAO to pursue the system with all the means he had at his disposal and sought additional contribution from interested governments and organizations for the implementation. Thus, in August 1973, the first issue of AGRINDEX was brought out on a cooperative basis. AGRIS is a computer based decentralized system with FAO as coordinating centre responsible for receiving, integrating, and processing bibliographic data submitted by national and regional centres all over the world.

In July 1974, the Government of India formally decided to participate in AGRIS Programme on a national basis through a national input centre under the Indian Council of Agricultural Research (ICAR). After an initial experimental carried out in November 1974, the Agricultural Research Information Centre (ARIC) began sending bibliographic data on AGRIS input sheets on a regular basis from May 1975 to the AGRIS data base at Vienna.

INSDOC

SDI Service

CHEM/SDI information retrieval system was started in January 1976 with Chemical Abstracts Condensates (CAC) and the CAN/SDI software by INSDOC, New Delhi, at IIT, Madras, with the support of UNESCO. The DST provided additional financial support under the NISSAT programme. Presently it is being run by the INSDOC's Regional Centre of Madras using the IBM 370/155 computer facility at IIT Madras. The INSPEC and COMPNEDEX data bases were also added later.

On-line Service

RECON On-line Demonstration : For the first time in Asia, an on-line interactive computer demonstration of the ESRIN/RECON data base system at Frascati, Italy was arranged at the Tata Institute of Fundamental Research (TIFR), Bombay from 20 to 25 September 1976. The satellite communication segment between Bombay and Rome was used for on-line linkage. It was done with the financial support of UNESCO. About 700 scientists, engineers and others participated in this demonstration. The users could communicate with the data base being searched by using an interactive terminal.

NIC

Information System for Planning : The National Informatics Centre (NIC) under the Electronics Commission is responsible for establishment and development of computerized information system for planning. To achieve this NIC has built an intra-city computer network (NICNET) in Delhi by connecting six minicomputer terminals to the host Cyber-170 computer system using leased telephone lines and radio (VHF) frequencies. It has also planned to establish four data bases initially in the fields of A. Agriculture; B. Financial information; C. Manpower information; and D. Industry and technology. It has planned to provide 60 interactive terminals in the various central and states government departments and ministries for on-line access. These Management Information Systems will be helpful for planning and policy making.

Data Communication

APPLE Experiment: APPLE (Ariane Passenger Payload Experiment), India's first experimental communication satellite was orbitted in 1981. It has a three-axis stabilized platform, an apogee motor and a C-band communication system. The National Informatics Centre has successfully conducted the Delhi-Ahmedabad satellite data communication experiment using APPLE. Large earth stations erected at Delhi, Ahmedabad, and Madras were used for computer interconnect experiments through APPLE.

INDONET : The Computer Maintenance Corporation (CMC) had an ambitious project in the area of communication, INDONET, which envisaged the establishment of a grid of computer centres with adequate intercommunication facilities and sophisticated hardware for advanced data processing. A design of message-switching system with store and forward facilities for teleprinters named AUTOMEX has been successfully completed. These systems are of great advantage for on-line information retrieval.

SITE Program : In 1975-76, the Indian Space Research Organization (ISRO) carried out a short-term Satellite Instructional Television Experiment (SITE) with the help of USA's ATS-6 satellite loaned to India for a period of one year to evaluate the feasibility of providing satellite television to selected rural areas in the country. This was one of the largest satellite based mass communication projects ever undertaken. Direct reception TV sets were provided to 2400 villages spread over six states. SITE was designed as a total communication systems experiment involving the hardware delivery system consisting of the satellite, earth stations, studios, ground receivers and various links as well as the concomitant software system consisting of formative research, program production, evaluation and feedback.

Satellite Telecommunictions Experiment Project: The Satellite Telecommunications Experiment Project (STEP) was large-scale demonstration experiment conducted in 1977-79 using the Franco-German Satellite SYMPHONIE. The aim of this experiment was to gain experience in the field of domestic satellite telecommunication. Under the project, experiments in digital satellite communications, radio networking and television transmission were carried out.

PROGRAMMES

UNISIST

The idea of establishing a world system of scientific information which later became UNISIST originated in India. At the Eleventh General Conference of the International Council of Scientific Unions (ICSU) held in Bombay in

January 1966, a proposal was adopted to create a committee to examine the feasibility of a world scientific information system based upon achieving compatibility among existing and prospective programmes related to the storage and retrieval of science information. By then UNESCO was also considering proposals for convening an International conference on the transfer of scientific and technological information. Realizing the need for cooperation for achieving the best results, the two organizations came together and created a UNESCO/ICSU Central Committee in January 1967 to carry out a feasibility study for a world science information system. After a three-years study, the committee submitted its study report in October 1970. The result was the establishment of UNISIST.

India and UNISIST

India has been actively participating in some of the UNISIST programmes right from the beginning. She was a member of the Steering Committee of UNISIST. Neelameghan of DRTC, Bangalore was also Chairman of the UNISIST Advisory Committee. India had hosted the Second UNISIST Meeting of Experts on Regional Information Policy and Planning in South and Central Asia in New Delhi from 18th March to 20th March 1976. Following this, the UNESCO Regional Seminar on Scientific, Technical and Industrial information Services was organized by INSDOC, New Delhi from 22nd March to 23rd March 1976. The Seminar felt the need for a Regional Task Group for developing and monitoring of regional programmes in library and information science. A Seminar, "Library and Information Science Manpower Development in the Asian Region' was organized by the DRTC in collaboration with UNESCO from 9th to 12th November, 1976. Further a short course on Scientific Editing for editors from countries covered by UNESCO/ROSTSCA was held in New Delhi from 8th to 16th November, 1976.

NISSAT

Realising the urgency for a strong national information system, India made an appeal to UNESCO for a short-term mission of a consultant to advise the INSDOC in these matters. Accordingly, UNESCO deputed Dr. Peter Lazar during March-April 1972, who, after a thorough study, recommended the establishment of a National Information System for Science and Technology (NISSAT) for India. The Panel Group on the Information Sector of the National Committee on Science and Technology (NCST) of the Government of India in its report, prepared in 1973, also recommended the establishment of NISSAT under the Department of Science and Technology (DST) Plan for 1974-79. A sum of Rs. 150 million was proposed for this scheme during the plan period. As a result, the planning of NISSAT was started in 1975 and was completed and approved by the Planning Commission and the Ministry of Finance for implementation since July, 1977. Its activities have been suspended recently.

DEVELOPMENTS IN 1980s

National Centre for Telematics

In the Doordarshan news telecasted on 16th April 1984, it was announced that the Government of India will shortly establish a National Centre for Telematics in New Delhi which was envisaged to initiate systems for data, facsimile, teletext, videotext, telemail transmission in the country.

INDITEXT

'Inditext': The Delhi Doordarshan introduced the home information system in Delhi on an experimental basis from 14th November 1985. This service called "Inditext" (Indian teletext) is available from 6 a.m. till midnight. The equipment was installed successfully at Doordarshan by Electronics Corporation of India Ltd. (ECIL), a public sector undertaking. It has also designed, developed and installed 100 receiver sets in the capital. The software was provided by the National Informatics Centre (NIC).

Just at the press of a button on a small Keypad (the size of a hand calculator) called decades a viewer can command his TV set to project Inditext or the normal programme. And if he does not want to disturb the normal programme, the teletext could be superimposed.

Various categories of information selected for transmission include index, news, financial news, sports news, TV Choice, TV tomorrow, whether information, airlines, railways, city engagements, cinemas, travel information, quiz, etc.

DOT (Department of Telecommunication)

Creation of MTNL and VSNL

In 1985, the administration of Rajiv Gandhi introduced the first significant institutional reform in the sector. Telecommunication services were separated from postal services, the DoT was created under the jurisdiction of the Ministry of Communications to provide telecom services, and the Telecom Board (now the Telecom Commission) was formed to develop policy for the sector. In 1986, further restructuring led to the creation of two new companies : Mahanagar Telephone Nigam Ltd. (MTNL) and Videsh Sanchar Nigam Ltd. (VSNL). While VSNL took charge of DoT international operations, MTNL took over the Department's local services in Bombay and New-Delhi.

Currently services are provided by the DoT, MTNL and VSNL, but both MTNL and VSNL are under the institutional umbrella of the DoT. Policy is drafted through a complicated and some obscure process in which the Ministry of Communications, the Telecom Commission, and the DoT have say. Institutional boundaries and policy making responsibilities are not clearly carried among these institutions. Although the Telecom Commission has the upper hand on regulatory recommendations, the actual implementation of policies is usually the outcome of political margin that involves not only these three institutions but also the Prime Minister's office, the Ministry of Finance, and the Parliament. As in the most democracies, these institutions often disagree on policies, slowing down any reform initiatives but providing legitimacy to the legislation that is implemented.

To de-politicize the current regulatory process somewhat, the government has passed a law transferring all regulatory functions in the sector to an autonomous regulatory body, the Telecom Regulatory Authority of India. This new agency is a non-statutory body operating under the jurisdiction of the Ministry of Communications, but it will presumably have considerable power and independence to buffer political influences from the executive branch, Parliament and other interest groups. The Authority's main tasks will include regulating everyday service provision and carrier operations, mediating among carriers and between carriers and customers, and enforcing legislation. More specifically, it will address issues related to standards for technical compatibility of networks and applications, pricing mechanisms and regimes and interconnection-related matters such as revenue-sharing agreements, access charges and time frames for interconnection.

OPTICAL/LASER DISCS

Optical/Laser discs brought yet another revolution in information and communication technologies. The use of online retrieval of bibliographic databases has reduced drastically with the use of CDs.

CD-ROM

Laser discs are one of read-only, write-once, or erasable and also one of analogue or digital. Read-only optical or laser discs are inexpensive to produce and the data on the discs cannot be altered. These discs are suitable as a computer storage medium, specially when the information needs to be amended and updated. These are, however, suitable for electronic publication of documents and graphics. The readonly analogue version is useful for storing video images and can hold digital data by converting it to analogue data.

Write-Once-Discs

Write-Once-Discs or WORMs (Write-Once-Read-Many) otherwise known as DRAW (Direct-Read-After-Write) have drives with a higher power laser than read-only. These discs can store digital files from work processor, documents, engineering and computer aided design drawings.

Erasable Discs

These will enable to erase a record, add new information, modify an existing *one* or manipulate the information in a way *one* needs. These will offer a much larger storage capacity than magnetic discs.

INTERNET

History of the Internet

During 1969 the US Department of Defence, through their Advanced Research Project Agency (ARPA) created an experiment. This was a Packet Switched Network over telephone lines. Out of this initial network Advanced Research Project Agency Network (ARPANET) one of the early forerunners of Internet was born. During 1970s the ARPA developed a set of rules, called protocols, that helped in connecting different networking connected to ARPANET continued to grow over the years. In 1982 ARPANET joined with MILNET (The Military Network) and a few others and it is said that the internet was thus formed from this consolidation of networks. As per the information available, there are 2,20,00,00 users by 1995 on the internet, and every month 1,50,000 new users are joining it. It is estimated that by the end of the year 2009, there will be 20 crore users on the Internet.

Uses of Internet

The Internet today gives access to an overwhelming amount of information, data and electronic information services provided by its ordinary users. At one end of the spectrum, there are personal 'home pages' published by people the world over (for name-searchable collection see *Ahoy : The Homepage Gateway).* At the other end is official government information, for example, that provided by the *open-gov.uk* website, which provides a first point of entry for all UK government and public sector information.

To give a few examples, the Internet can be used to :

- exchange personal messages with colleagues, friends or relatives at other networked sites,
- engage in group discussions, exchange inform ation and ideas with people who share a common interest, and seek information from them,
- automatically receive information on world eve nts, leisure interests, and technical, business and professional matters by subscribing to electronic journals, conferences, newsletters and alerting services,
- look up information in reference works, databases and libraries worldwide,
- retrieve journal articles, books, computer progr ams, and graphic images, and transfer them to a personal computer,
- make use of computer facilities that are not available locally,
- download new software or updates for existing

applications,

- browse catalogues of goods and services and make credit-card purchases,
- participate in distance learning and academic conferencing,
- engage in read-time 'chat' and multiplayer interactive games,
- communicate with individuals or groups by means of voice only or voice and image, and
- publish information for access by other internet users.

WWW (=World Wide Web) : Documents and Links

The WWW began as an attempt to link researchers at CERN, the European Laboratory for Particle Physics, in Geneva, Switzerland. Around the same time that the Gopher and WAIS software were being developed, a small group of developers led by Tim. Bemers-Lee at CERN proposed a network-based hypertext system for use at the institute.

The web combines two ideas which alone are useful and together have proven to be extraordinarily powerful: networked information and hypertext. By the time of its development, a number of systems that provided users access to networked information were available, anonymous FTP servers being the earliest and most used. Gopher being extremely approachable and opening up the world of networked information to many new users, and WAIS introduced many users to a full-text search engine for a networked retrieval system.

However, none of these systems provided a method of linking one piece of information directly to another within the body of a document. Such links are called hyperlinks and are a distinguishing feature of hypertext. Indeed, hypertext can be defined simply as a system of links of nodes, where the nodes may be documents that contain such links.

The WWW is a set of protocols that (i) allow for the location of any document on the Net through a naming system based on Universal Resource Locators (URLs); (ii) describe a way of placing links using URLs within text documents, called Hypertext Markup Language (HTML); and (iii) specify a way to request and send a document over the network, the Hypertext Transfer Protocol (HTTP). With these standard protocols in place, one can set up a server and construct the responsibility of making the users aware of their role in fair use of the electronic access to the journals. Davis and Reilly (1998) believe that the licensing of electronic journals requires legal expertise and skills beyond the training and experience of most librarians.

ELECTRONIC JOURNALS - INDIAN SCENARIO

In India, many research libraries and some university libraries are already accessing the electronic counterpart of the printed journals, which they are subscribing to. Most of these journals have the online access free along with the print subscription. For the last two or three years, many publishers and vendors were experimenting with their different pricing strategies to the libraries in India. Some of them started the offer of online access to the electronic journals free on a trial basis, wherever the libraries were subscribing to their print versions. As a next step, a few publishers offered their electronic journals for a nominal fee in addition to the print journals. The publishers were trying to arrive at a price, suitable to the libraries, especially for those in the developing countries (Louis, *et al.*, 2001).

While the libraries in North America and Europe were accessing the online journals, the libraries in India were still struggling to set up the infrastructure required for online access to journals. As a result, there is a delay in acquiring the electronic journals and databases in Indian libraries. Additionally, our library budgets do not give the flexibility to buy the much-required high-tech format of the information. Librarians are in a fix, as to how to manage accessing information within their budget. In addition, they are also expected to bargain for accessing more information. This is precisely what libraries in other countries have managed by establishing some formal networks like consortia, which have the ability to bargain collectively with the commercial publishers. The same concept or the trend has spread to our country in recent times. More and more publishers have shown interest and willingness to have a dialog with librarians in India. They expect the librarians to have a formal commitment among themselves before they start bargaining with the publishers. In the absence of standardized formal consortia arrangements within the country, it is a difficult situation for Indian libraries to accept the existing procedure for consortia models in other countries.

CONSORTIA APPROACH

Consortia are nothing but cooperative effort, which manages all the library services collectively. It has the purpose of exploring the need for libraries to make the most effectiveness of their funds collectively. This partnership fosters pride, determination and a sense of ownership between its constituent libraries and staff. Consortia are regarded as an effective strategy to increase the buying power of individual libraries over the short term and as an opportunity to maximize the efforts of cooperative collection building for resource sharing over the long term (Richer, 1999). It is essential to understand the definition of the term "consortium" which is a powerful cooperative strategy.

The following definitions from the available sources are the derivation from the basic term of "consortium".

A Consortium is said to be "a cooperative arrangement among groups or institutions, or an association or society"

(American Heritage Dictionary)

Consortia in India

Libraries are taking the consortia to which they belong a great deal more seriously, than was the case a few years back. They offer libraries the ability to give users the access they are coming to expect and demand to a much broader range of materials than any one library could possibly offer.

Some of the Indian Consortia

1. FORSA (forum for Resource Sharing in Astronomy).
2. INDEST (Indian Digital Library in Engineering Science and Technology).
3. IIM Consortium.
4. UGC's INFONET.
5. CSIR Consortium.

OPEN ACCESS JOURNALS

Due to rapid growth in ICT, there has been tremendous scope to publish articles in a new breed of media, i.e. Open Access Journals (OAJ). The basic criteria of OAJ is to be available freely on the Web to any one to read, download, to save and down load either on Institutional Archives or Central Archives with no barriers of any kind. There are journals with online access but majority of them are accessible only on subscription. It has been estimated that there are about 5% of scholarly publishing journals which follow open access model. It is to be noted that OA journals also follow all rigorous treatment of peer review as of non-OA journals.

Characteristics of open access journals

The characteristics of open access journals as identified by Suber, P (2005) are :

- OA journals conduct peer review;
- OA journals typically let authors retain copyright;

- OA journals levy fee from the authors or his employer;
- Some OA journal publishers are not-for-profit (e.g. PLoS) and some are for-profit (e.g. BioMed Central or BMC); and
- OA journals are economically viable and dissem inate information at a faster rate;

Indian Digital Repositories

Following institutions have developed institutional repositories in India :

1. Indian Institute of Astrophysics;
2. IIM, Kozhikode;
3. Indian Institute of Science (IISc), Bangalore;
4. Indian Statistical Institute (ISI), Bangalore;
5. INFLIBNET, Ahmedabad;
6. Information Centre for Aerospace Science and Technology (ICAST);
7. National Chemical Laboratory (NCL);
8. National Informatics Centre (NIC), Delhi;
9. National Institute of Oceanography (NIO);
10. National Institute of Technology, Rourkela;
11. One World South Asia (OWSA);
12. Raman Research Institute, Bangalore;
13. University of Delhi, etc.

NATIONAL KNOWLEDGE COMMISSION

NKC is composed of honorary member of eminence, scholarship, academic and professional achievements, scientists and technologists with expertise in management and persons of vast experience, under the chairmanship of Dr Sam Pitroda of International reputation. The names of the other members are : Dr. P M Bhargava (Vice-Chairman), Dr: Ashok Ganguly, Dr Jyaniti Ghosh,, Dr. Deepak Nayyar,

Dr. Nandan Nilekani, Dr Andre Betille and Dr. Pratap Bhanu Mehta. Established on 13th June 2005, NKC had time frame of three years from 2nd October 2005 to 2nd October 2008 to achieve its objectives.

The organisation structure of NKC is given in Fig. 1.

Prime Minister

↓

Planning Commission ↔ Chairman ↔ Ministries/States

↓

Members

↓

Support Staff

Fig. 1

NKC will be assisted by Technically Support Staff, Officers on Special Duty, a National Steering Group under the Chairmanship of PM. The group includes the Ministers of Human Resources Development, Agriculture, Commerce and Industry and Communication and Information Technology, State Minister of Science and Technology and the Deputy Chairman of the Planning Commission.

Three Advisers to assist NKC in their tasks are for Open and Distance Education, Public Information.

NKC Objectives

The overall task before NKC is to take steps that will give India the 'Knowledge edge' in the coming decades, i.e. to ensure that our country becomes a leader in the creation, application and dissemination of knowledge.

- *Creation of new* knowledge principally depends on strengthening the education system, promoting domestic research and innovation in laboratories as well as at the grass roots level and tapping ; foreign sources of knowledge through more open trading regimes, foreign investment and technology, licensing;

- *Application of* knowledge will primarily target the sectors of health, agriculture, government and industry. This involves diverse priorities like using traditional knowledge in agriculture, enco uraging innovation in industry and agriculture and building a strong governance framework for public services;
- *Dissemination* of knowledge focuses on ensuring universal elementary education, especially for girls and other traditionally disadvantaged group, creating a culture of lifelong learning especially for skilled workers, taking steps to boost literacy levels, and using information and communication technology (ICT) to enhance standards in educat ion and widely disseminate easily accessible knowledge that is useful to the public.

REFERENCES

1. Kumar, PSG. Computerization of Indian Libraries. New Delhi BRPC, 1978.
2. Kumar, PSG. Fundamentals of information Science. Ed. 3. Delhi. Indraprastha, 2008.
3. Kumar, PSG. Information technology : Basics. New Delhi : BRPC, 2003.

11
Electronic Resources and Services*

STORAGE DEVICES

Optical/Laser Discs

Optical/Laser discs brought yet another revolution in information and communication technologies. The use of online retrieval of bibliographic databases has reduced drastically with the use of CDs.

CD-ROM

Laser discs are one of read-only, write-once, or erasable and also one of analgoue or digital. Readonly optical or laser discs are expensive to produce and the data on the discs cannot be altered. These discs are suitable as a computer storage medium, specially when the information needs to be amended and updated. These are, however, suitable for electronic publication of documents and graphics. The read

* Keynote Address delivered at the National Seminar on "Impact of ICT on Library and Its Services" held at Dr. Babasaheb Ambedkar College, Brahmapuri on 8 Feb. 2011.

only analogue version is useful for storing video images and can hold digital data by converting it to analogue data.

INTERNET

The Internet has revolutionised our society, our economy and our technological systems. Over the past century, important technological developments have created a global environment that is drawing people of the world closer and closer together. About fifteen years ago, most of the world knew little or nothing about the Internet. The Internet was then a private network accessible only to computer scientists and researchers who used it to interact with colleagues in their respective disciplines. It is estimated that about 60 million host computers on the Internet today serve about 200 million users in over 200 countries and territories. Also, the total numbers of host computers and users have been growing at about 33% every six months since 1988-or roughly 80% per year.

INTERNET-BASED COMMUNICATION SERVICES

Libraries use Internet-based Communication system while attending their day-to-day routine works. An Internet-based Communication System allows communication between computer users hooked into a network. Internet-based Communication System is used for communication between person-to-person, person-to-group and group-to-group. A document or message sent through electronic system may contain text, graphics, image, speech as well as other types of information. Major Internet-based communication services are described below.

E-mail

Electronic Mail, or e-mail, is a fast, easy and inexpensive way to communicate with other internet users around the world. It is the most popular and widely used services of the Internet. E-mail is the term given to an electronic message, usually a form of simple text message that a user types at a computer system and is transmitted over some from of computer network to another user, who can read it. Email offers speedy and economical transfer of messages anywhere in the world.

Listservs

Listservs are electronic groups that typically centre around broad topics such as Digital Libraries or Reference Service, etc. Listservs of IFLA with the name IFLA-1, Digilib-1, LIBJOBS-1 are good example of this. Every e-mail message sent to the Listserv is distributed to all members of that listserv, which is potentially hundreds or thousands of people. It does not cost anything *to* subscribe to a listerver.

Chat or Instant Messangers

Chat refers to any live discussions conducted using the Internet, usually between more than two persons using their keyboard to communicate. Chat programs allow users on the Internet to communicate with each other by typing in real time. It is a feature offered by many online serves or Web sitest that allows users to "Chat" by typing messages which are displayed almost instantly on the screens of other users who are using the chat room at a given time.

A variation of chat is the phenomenon of the instant messenger. Instant messaging can be used to ¦ communicate privately with friends, relatives or co-workers. To send and receive instant messages, a user needs a connection to the Internet and instant messaging software such as Gmai! Messenger, Yahoo Messenger and MSN Messanger.

Conferencing

One of the most exciting features of internet is to communicate, talk, and see groups of people in different locations around the world, without the expense of travel. Conferencing can take many forms, such as web chat, audio conferencing, video conferencing, multimedia conferencing, screen-sharing, etc. The conferencing programs, such as the popular CU-SeeMe, allow workgroups to use the Internet to see each others' faces in small windows on the computer screen and to hear their voices through computer speakers. One can use desktop video and audio simultaneously or audio can be used alone or just use the screen-sharing capability without either audio or video.

1. Audio-Conferencing & Internet Telephone : Internet telephony also called IP telephony is a combination of hardware arid software that allows the Internet to be used as a telephone carrier. Internet telephony is the conversion of analogue speech signals used on current telephone systems into digital data, allowing calls to be sent over the internet, bypassing long distance charges. While the Internet was first devised as a way of transmitting data, it is now being used to make voice calls.

2. Video Conferencing : Video conferencing is one of the most exciting areas of development in telecommunications, with applications ranging from business to government to education to home and family. Video conferencing involves sending video signals as well as audio and computer data signals. Conferencing can be done one-to-one, one-to many (called multicast), and many-to-many (called multipoint). While video conferencing, one can talk as well as see the people sitting miles away as if all are discussing in one room facing each other. One of the most popular applications is transmission of news from various locations by the TV news channels.

Net Meeting

Microsoft NetMeeting facilities a new way of talking, meeting, working and sharing over the internet. It uses internet phone voice communications and conferencing standards to provide multi-user applications and data sharing over intranets or the Internet. Two or more users can work together and collaborate to reach at a time using application sharing, whiteboard, and chat functionality.

News Groups

Another Internet service similar to listservs is a newsgroup. News Groups are like an International bulletin board. Each group is a forum for a different subject, where a subscriber can post his / her questions or answers. There are thousands of groups covering just about every area of interest. The difference between listserv and news groups is that when a user joins a group, the mail is no longer automatically deposited into his mailbox. Instead a user is expected to go to the newsgroup himself to read it.

INTERNET-BASED CONTENT PUBLISHING AND DELIVERY SERVICES

The World Wide Web-known as WWW, W3 or simply, the Web help people to publish, organize and provide access to information on the Internet. The WWW can be defined as a hypertext, multimedia, distributed information system that provides links to hypertext documents, as well as to man other internet tools and databases. The Web serves as a platform for several specialised content publishing and delivery services.

Some of the important tools for content publishing and delivery services applicable *to* libraries and information centres are described below.

Blogs

A blog (an abridged from of term web log) is a website, usually maintained by an individual, with regular entries of commentary, descriptions of events, or other material such as graphics or video. Entries are commonly displayed in reverse chronological order (Wikipedia, 2008). Blogs are considered as lightweight publishing tools. Blogs provide control to an individual or group of individuals for publishing contents or making commentary on it.

Wikis

A wiki is a collection of web pages deigned to enable anyone who accesses it to contribute or modify content, using a simplified markup language. Wikis are often used to create collaborative websites and to power community websites (Wikipedia, 2008). For example, the collaborative encylopaedia, Wikipedia is one of the best-know wikis that has broken down one of the golden rules of librarianship, i.e. content validation and authenticity of information. Wikis are also used in businesses to provide affordable and effective Intranets and for knowledge management. Ward Cunningham, developer of the first Wiki software, WikiWiki Web, orginally described it as "the simplest online database that could possible work" (Wikipedia, 2008).

Podcasting

The word "Podcasting" is derived from two words, namely "Broadcasting" and "iPod" (popular MP3 player from Apple Computer). Podcasting is defined as "Process of capturing audio digital-media files that can be distributed over the Internet using RSS feeds for playing-back on portable media players as well as computers. Users can subscribe to such feeds and automatically download these files directly into an audio management program (such as Itunes, Windows Media Player or MusicMatch) on their PCs. When a user synchronize their portable audio device with their personal computer the podcasts are automatically transferred to that device to be listened to at the time and location most convenient for the user (Wikipedia, 2008).

Vodcasting

The "VOD" in Vodcasting stands for "Video-on-demand". It is identical to podcasting. While podcasting is used for delivering audio filed, vodcasting is used for delivering video content. Like podcast content, vodcasts content can be played either on a laptop or on personal media assistant (PMA).

RSS Feeds

RSS stands for Real Simple Syndication or Rich Site Summary. The technology, on one hand allows a web site (or e-publisher) to list the newest published updates (like table of contents of journals, new articles); through a technology called XML, on the other hand, it facilitates a web user to keep track new updates on chosen website (s). Like a personal search assistant, RSS feed readers visit pre-defined web sites, look for updated information and fetch it automatically on to the user's desktop. It provides users a way to syndicate and republish content on the Web. Users repulish content from other sites or blogs on their sites or blogs, aggregate content on other sites in a single place, and ostensibly distil the Web for their personal use.

ELECTRONIC RESOURCES

Electronic resources can be defined as resources in electronic format or computer-processible format that provide information or an indicator to the information and are generally accessible over the internet or stored on media like CD-ROM/DVD-ROM or other storage devices. The emergence of Internet and the World Wide Web (WWW) in early 1990s, as a new media of information storage and delivery, came as a real boon for evolution of electronic resources.

Electronic Databases

An electronic database consists of electronic resources integrated in highly organized fashion so as to provide controlled access to it by their commercial providers. The first databases were bibliographic in nature and were online version of existing indexing and abstracting services such as *Biological Abstracts, Index Medicus, Chemical Abstracts,* etc. By the year 1988, only half of all databases were bibliographic in nature. With introduction of a number of online databases containing textual information, news, statistics, commodity prices, etc., a third type of databases holding text of full-length documents started appearing. Several full-text of encyclopaedia, directories and articles from journals are now available online. Most of the ' publishers now provide access to their full-text journals through their web site or through other electronic publishing platforms. While these are a number of public-domain data-bases, most online database require annual subscription for accessing them. Thousands of databases are now available on compact discs (CD-ROM) as well as on the Web.

Electronic Journals

Electronic journals, or "e-journals", are used for those journals and newsletters that are prepared and distributed electronically. Electronic journals may be defined very broadly as any journal, magazine, e-zine, webzine, newsletter or type of electronic serial publication which is available over the internet and can be , accessed using different technologies such as WWW, Gopher, ftp, telnet, e-mail or listserv. Several traditional journals are now being published both on the Web and in print. Content lists for most the journals are available on the Web or distributed to subscribers as an e-mail text messages or through technologies like RSS and Atom.

Internet-based electronic journals started to appear in the beginning of 1990. These journals were mostly delivered as an attachment to e-mail while their back issues were mounted on anonymous ftp sites and users were required and information centres made them accessible through their gopher site. 1995 witnessed peak of Gopher technology which then dropped suddenly and dramatically by 1997. With advent of WWW technology in 1993, electronic publishing became more than a novelty, the web as a means of delivery of electronic information has grown steadily since then. As publishers experiment with different publication modes and models, the very definition of a journal is undergoing change in the electronic environment. New journals have evolved based on the graphic capabilities of the Internet that are available only in electronic form.

Like print journals, current and archival issues of electronic journals can be browsed through their content pages. Moreover, e-journals can also be searched not only on their metadata but also in full-text through sophisticated search interface. Currently, there are more than 50,000 peer-reviewed, scholarly electronic journals that are available on the Internet.

Electronic Books

An electronic book is digital reading material that a user can view on a desktop or Personal Digital Assistant (PDA), laptop or on a dedicated, portable device with a large storage capacity and the ability to download new titles via a network connection. More and more traditional book publishers, as well as those catering to the professional and business communities, are launching their e-book collections.

The electronic books market consists of two distinct components i.e. (i) electronic books consisting of digital material or contents; and (ii) electronic book hardware including e-book reading appliances, PCs. laptop or PDA. The digital material or content that make an electronic book are simply textual and graphical files consisting of bits that can be transported any digital storage media or delivered over a network connection. It is designed to be viewed on some combination of hardware and software ranging from dumb terminals to web browers, on personal computers to the new reading appliances.

More and more books are now being released on the web through enhanced interfaces that offer features such as increased search capacity within a book or entire collection of books, ability to highlight and flag a page, ability to make notes on text without damaging the book, ability to e-mail quotes from the books to other colleagues, etc. Most publishers like Springer, Wiley Interscience, Taylor and Francis, Cambridge University Press, Oxford University Press, etc. offer their e-book collections on subscription/one-time purchase basis. Besides, there are a number of e-books aggregators that make thousands of books available online for libraries and individuals at relatively lower cost. Three major e-books aggregators aer Questia (http:www.questia.com),Ebrary(http://www.ebrary.com/) and NetLibrary (http:/www.netlibrary.com/). However, i just like other e-resources, e-books come with restrictions such as limit on downloads, in terms of number of pages, i.e. one page at a time or one chapter at a time or no download at all.

Electronic Theses and Dissertations

Theses submitted to the universities as requirement for the award of Ph.D. degree constitute a useful source of information for the new and ongoing research. Doctoral dissertations submitted to universities and academic institutions are orignally created in digital format using one of the word processing software packages like MS Word, Latex, Word Perfect, Word Pro, etc. or one of the desktop publishing packages like Page Maker, Ventura, etc. These documents are undisputedly highly valuable collection especially in digital format that qualify to be an important component of a digital library. The documents composed on word processing packages / desktop publishing packages can be easily concerted into PDF, Post Script or XML using appropriate software tools so as to host them on the web. Serval universities and institutions have already implemented electronic submission of doctoral dissertations under the overall umbrella of an international digital library initiative called "Networked Digital Library of Theses and Dissertations" (NDLTD).

Digitized Print Material

Several digital library projects are concerned with providing digital access to materials that already exists with traditional libraries in printed media. Scanned page images are practically the only reasonable solution for institutions such as libraries for converting existing paper collection (legacy documents) without having access to the original data in computer processible formats convertible into HTML/XML or in any other structured or unstructured text. Scanned page images are natural choice for large-scale conversions for major digital library initiatives. Printed text, pictures and figures are transformed into computer accessible forms using a digital scanner or a digital camera in a process called document imaging or scanning. The digitally scanned images are stored in a files as a bit-mapped page image, irrespective of the fact that a scanned page contains a photograph, a line drawing or text.

Audio, Video and Streaming Media

Streaming multimedia is sequential delivery of multimedia content, including video, audio or some other learning objects, over a computer network that is displayed (or played back) to the end-user as it is being delivered by the provider. The advent of the MP3 players and the iPod resulted in a greater effort to deliver downloadable media. Moreover, web documents are now coming with greater integration of text with media. Encyclopaedia are now have articles with audio files, video clips and animation to illustrate a given topic.

SUBJECT GATEWAYS OR LIBRARY PORTALS

The web, being a hypermedia-based system, allows linking amongst electronic resources stored on servers dispersed geographically on distant locations. The portal sites or gateways redirect a user to the holders of the original digital material. The librarians, being the earliest users of the web, started to gather and organize link to important web-based resources on various subjects.

A subject gateway can be defined as facilities that allow easier access to web-based resources in a defined subject area. The simplest types of subject gateways are sets of web pages containing list of links to resources. Some gateways index their lists of links and provides a simple search facility. More advanced gateways offer a much-enhanced service via a system consisting of a resource database and various indexes, which can be search and or browse throughout a web-based interface. (O' Leary, 2000).

WWW(=World Wide Web): Documents and Links

The WWW began as an attempt link researchers at CERN, the European Laboratory for Particle Physics, in Geneva, Switzerland. Around the same time that the Gopher and WAIS software were being developed, a small group of developers led by Tim. Bemers-Lee at CERN proposed a network-based hypertext system for use at the institute.

The Web combines two ideas which alone are useful and together have proven to be extraordinarily powerful : net-worked information and hypertext. By the time of its development, a number of systems that provided users access to networked information were available, anonymous FTP servers being the earliest and most used. Gopher being extremely approachable and opening up the world of net-worked information to many new users, and WAIS introduced many users to a full-text search engine for a networked retrieval system.

However, none of these systems provided a method of linking one piece of information directly to another within the body of a document. Such links are called hyperlinks and are a distinguishing feature of hypertext. Indeed, hypertext can be define simply as a system of links of nodes, where the nodes may be documents that contain such links.

The WWW is a set of protocols that (i) allow for the location of any document on the Net through a naming system based on Universal Resource locators (URLs); ii) describe a way of placing links using URLs within text documents, called Hypertext Markup Language (HTML); and (iii) specify a way to request and send a document over the network, the Hypertext Transfer Protocol (HTTP). With these standard protocols in place. one can set up a server and construct the responsibility of making the users aware of their role in fair use of the electronic access to the journals. Davis and Reilly (1998) believe that the licensing of electronic journals requires legal expertise and skills beyond the training and experience of most librarians.

INFORMATION TECHNOLOGY BASED LIBRARY SERVICES

New information technology can potentially support a range of traditional and non-traditional library ' services. Most of the library services generated using information technology resemble closely to those generated manually with improvements and modifications to suit the requirements of automated services. Examples of some of IT-based library services are given below.

OPAC and WebPAC

Remote access to the Library catalogues (OPAC) was possible only through a telnet connection before the Web (www.telecampus.edu/) lists more than 12,000 online courseware available on the web. Moreover, highly specialized web sites are now coming-up in various disciplines which offer information in totality including all kind of resources in electronic format, EI Engineering Village (http:/www.ei.org/), ISI Electronic Library (http://www.isinet.com), BEEE/IEE Electronic Library (http://www.ieee.org/), Engineering Sciences Data Unit (http:/www.esdu.com) are some of the important examples.

Digitzed Documents

Several digital library projects are concerned with providing digital access to materials that already exists with traditional libraries in printed media. Digitization of printed material is practically the only reasonable solution for institutions such as libraries for converting existing paper collection (legacy documents) without having access to the original data in computer processible formats. Digitization is the natural choice for large-scale conversions for major digital library initiatives. Printed text, pictures and figures are transformed into computer-accessible forms using a digital scanner or a digital camera in a process called document imaging or scanning. The digitally scanned images are stored in a file as a bit-mapped page image, irrespective of the fact that a scanned page contains a photograph, a line drawing or text. A bit-mapped page image is a type of computer graphic, literally an electronic picture of the page which can most easily be equated to a facsimile image of the page and as such they can be read by humans, but not by the computers, understably "text" in a page image is not searchable on a computer using the present-day technology. An image-based implementation require a large space for data storage and transmission. There are several large projects using page images as their primary storage format, including project JSTOR (www.jstor.org) at Princeton University funded by the Melon Foundation. The project Jstor has a complete set of more than 1000+ journals scanned and hosted on web servers that resides at the University of Michigan and is mirrored at Princeton University. Using technology developed at Michigan, high resolution (600 dpi) bit-mapped image of each page are linked to a text file generated with optical character recognition (OCR) software. Linking a searchable text file to the page images of the entire published record of a journal along with newly constructed table of contents, indexes, permits high level of access, search and retrieval of the journal material previously unimaginable (Guthrie, 1997).,

Capturing page image format is comparatively easy and inexpensive. It is a faithful reproduction of its original maintaining page integrity and originality. The scanned textual images, however, are not searchable unless it is OCRed, which in itself, if highly error prone process specially when it involves scientific texts.

Open Access Journals

Due to rapid growth in ICT, there has been tremendous scope to publish articles in a new breed of media, i.e. Open Access Journals (OAJ). The basic criteria of OAJ is to be available freely on the Web to any one to read, download, to save and down load either on Institutional Archieves or Central Archives with no barriers of any kind. There are journals with online access but majority of them are accessible only on subscription. It has been estimated that there are about 5% of scholarly publishing journals which follow open access model. It is to be noted that OA journal also follow all rigorous treatment of peer review as of non-OA journals.

Characteristics of open access journals

The characteristics of open access journals as identified by Suber, P (2005) are:

- OA journals conduct peer review;
- OA journals typically let authors retain copyright;
- OA journals levy fee from the authors or his employer;
- Some OA journal publishers are not-for-profit (e.g. PLoS) and some are for-profit (e.g. BioMedCentral or BMC); and
- OA journals are economically viable and disseminate information at a faster rate;

LOCAL REPOSITORILES

Present scenario is of e-resources India is not far beyond so far as technical advancement is concerned. US professional should be ready with technological application in their work environment more especially with Internet and its attributes. As our role is defined we work as information intermediary. We must track the roots of information generation, distribution and dissemination. Virtually internet has become the only source of information store house, data mining and cultivation of information in the 21st century.

Self archieve

Self archive is a term which is defined in a way every information producer more simply who produces academic research papers, articles or any other write-ups should collect his/her own publications on the net. It is simply the one-line version of maintaining the files and folders in our personal computers. Certain tags or keywords can be given for indexing these archives. Mostly the name of scholar and his affiliation with the institutions.

Institutional Repository (IR)

Repository means formally organized and managed collection of digital content generated by faculty, staff and students at an institution. The main purpose of institutional repositories is to bring together and preserve the intellectual output of a laboratory, department and academic community.

IR is a set of services that an institute offers to the members of its community for the management and dissemination of digital materials created by the institution and its community. IR may contain the intellectual works of faculty and students-both research and teaching material and also documentation of the activities of the institution itself in the form of records of events and performance and of the ongoing intellectual life of the institution. IR may also contain experimental and observational data captured by members that supports scholarly activities and to preserve them and make them available to the members of their communities and to the public.

CONCLUSION

Need to Increase the Awareness of the Users

As per the survey on 'Perceptions of Libraries and Information Resources' undertaken by OCLC (www.oclc.org/reports/2005 perceptions.htm. Accessed on 14.1.2009), which surveyed the information seeking behaviour of over 3300 respondents, only 16% of respondents had ever used free search engines like Google. The report concludes, Majority of information seekers are not making much use of the array of information resources (online magazines, databases and reference assistance, for example) which libraries make available to the communities. The survey also showed that 39% of new information seekers learn about new electronic information sources through promotion or advertising as opposed to only 15% by message in the library sites. The librarian was ranked the lowest, at 8% as a source of information about e-resources.

One of the reasons for the slow uptake of e-resources is that its awareness among our users does not seem to be adequate as several studies indicate.

In a study of 143 faculty members in J.D. Institute of Engineering & Technology, Lohara, Mahrashtra in 2007,38% of faculty said that they were not using the e-joumals because of lack of awareness (Labhasettwar, 2007)

In a study of 300 faculty members from IIT Delhi and IIT Kanpur in 2007, 35.66% of faculty expressed the lack of awareness of e-journals in the Institute (Nisha and Naushad Ali, 2007).

In an another study conducted in six universities of

Karnataka state in which 845 research scholars participated, 37.86% of research scholars expressed the lack of awareness of e-journals (Gowda and Shivalingiah 2007).

In one more study of 378 post graduates and research students in B A Marathwada University, Aurangabad, 29% of research scholars said that they were not familiar with the concept of e-journals (Golwal, Sonwane and Vaishnav, 2007).

Therefore, increasing the awareness of e-resources is one of the initial steps to enhance their use.

Prediction about the future

As per a study commissioned by British Library, UK, it is estimated that by 2020, 40% of UK monographs will be available in exclusive electronic format while another 50% will be available in both print and digital. British Library predicts a switch over from print to digital publishing by the year 2020, with 90 percent of the British research monographs being published in electronic format by that date.

Promoting the Use

Various traditional methods are available and they continue to be effective. They are listed below.

1. A-Z lists of journals : Providing a list of e-journals subscribed and providing a direct link to the journals either from the library homepage or from the OPAC. This will ensure that the user does not miss out a particular periodical though it is hidden in a database. Such periodical list can be made alphabetically title wise.
2. Access e-books through library OPAC : Some Library automation packages do allow the integration of e-books metadata with library OPAC provided the metadata is in the standard format. Integration allows a single point of search both for print and e-books.

3. Subject guides compiled by the library staff comprising of evaluated printed and e-resources. These subject guides are put on the library website.

   E.g. University of Delware Library Subject Guides

   http:/www2.udel.edu/sub/(Accessed on 24.1.2009)

   http:/www.lib.ployu.edu.hk/(Accessed on 25.1.2009)

   Some libraries bring out course specific subject guides as given in the website. http:/library.csusm. edu/ guides.asp (Accessed 25.12009)

4. Banners, posters, brouchers, bookmarks, emails etc : Use of printed brouchers, flyers, posters, bookmarks etc should not be under estimated. Such flyers, brouchers, bookmarks etc be made freely available in various service points in the library. Posters be pinned in library, hostels, faculties meeting places etc. Various e-journal publishers have brought out templates of banners, posters, brouchures, bookmarks, e-mails and press releases which can be used for publicizing their e-books. These communication tool kits can be customized by putting your library logo, address etc.

REFERENCES

1. Arora, Jagdish, Information and communication technology (ICT), for Academic libraries. Jodhpur. scientific publishers, 2010. P-15-63.
2. Bhat, Ishwara. Marketing of e-Resources in University Libraries, Jodhpur, Scientific Publishers, 2010. P-91-107.
3. Kumar, PSG Computerization of Indian libraries. New Delhi. BRPC, 1987.
4. ...... Indian response to International development in ICT. Jodhpur: scientific Published, 2010. P-64-90.
5. ...... Knowledge organization, information processing and retrieval New Delhi. BRPC. 2003.
6. Rana, Madan Singh. Tracing e-resources through academic depositors for knowledge management. Johdpur: Scientific Publishers, 2010, P-186-197.

12

Planning Library Automation*

Let us define the scope of the topic to "Setting up a computer system for Library operations". It is assumed that we already know basic concepts of Computer-Hardware, Software data processing, programming, programming languages etc.

Stages

Thinking of this task as a *project,* we can discuss various aspects involved by looking at the several *stages* of Project Control Management.

1. Initial Study (Feasibility Study) (System Analysis)
2. Specifications of Requirements (Systems Analysis)
3. Design of the System (System design)
4. Development
5. Testing

---

* Text of a Lecture delivered at Academic Staff College, Osmania University, Hyderabad on 18 Nov. 1998.

6. Implementation
7. Running
8. Review.

Steps

We can think of the following steps in setting up a computer system for Library operations:

(a) Identifying the need and uses for the computer (stages 1, 2 6 & 7)
(b) Choosing the right computer and vendor
(c) Buying/installation/sitting/staffing etc.
(d) Putting computer to use: by carrying out various functional areas of library activity one by one, as identified in step (a) above (all stages)

There may be some overlapping of the stages without clear demarcation between stages. Generally all projects follow these common stages.

In this lectures we shall discuss stages 1,2,6 and 7 in detail with respect to "Computer choice, purchase, installation etc." and all stages in general with reference to "Computerisation of Library activities".

1. Initial Study

Initial study or Feasibility Study attempts to *Answer why do you need a Computer System?* The purpose of the initial study is to identify the reasons why computerisation should be undertaken in the first place (1) Results of the study will list areas of operation where speed and accuracy of a computer based system will be affordable, necessary or helpful; (2) There could be highly repetitive jobs requiring to be done fast and accurately; (3) The volume of Workload could have raised needing more clerical staff to be recruited; (4) There may be need for retrieval of information from large volumes of assorted data which is impossible by manual methods; and (5) Changes in technology may warrant the use of computers.

In the library environment several pieces of data (author or title for example) are repeatedly handled *ad-infinitum.*

Library is a growing organism. Collection grows. But staff position does not improve proportionately.

For instance—in the library area—reference books may be available only in CD-ROMS. Catalogue publications may be available only on Floppies or similar medium. Journals may be available in Electronic form etc.

2. System Analysis (Requirements Specification)

This stage of investigation answers the question "what must be achieved through computerisation"?

This is done by thorough investigation of all departments of the library, various procedures, forms/ registers, persons involved, flow of information, flow of work etc. Objectives as to what must be done are agreed upon with people concerned in specific terms. For example—"We should be able to send reminders for unsupplied books at least four times a year to every vendor".

Objectives : Formulation can be economic, technical, or social. "It should cut down cost of ordering activity by 50%".

"All programming will be done in dBASE II" (as we do not wish to recruit specialists for the task). No retrenchment may be allowed as a result of computerisation etc.

3. System Design

Here we try to answer—'"How do we achieve the objectives stated in detail in step 2" ?

Stages 1 and 2 are legwork and this design stage is brain work.

This is the most highly technical area where the System Analyst develops several models and decides on the best among the various alternative approaches to tackle the problem. He keeps in mind the organisation's constraints and user's requirements and balance judiciously.

How exactly data will be generated, validated, stored and made available for processing by the computer etc. are decided in this stage.

4. Development

Carrying out what has been decided in the 'Design' stage earlier, is development. In the case of Library Acquisition computerisation for example, this will involve writing of the program code, entering it into the computer, compiling, editing etc.

This job is the responsibility mainly that of the applications programmer.

In this stage, which may be longest if the programmes are developed inhouse, may call for a great deal of finer details.

Buying a ready made software package reduces this stage to a shortone. It is only needed to install, get trained, input data and start using the system.

5. Testing

Once the programme is written and checked out for syntax errors, it is tested.

The programmer answer the questions: "Will this programme ever work" ? in the first phase of testing. Then he obtains sample data as well as manually arrived at results (output) from the user. The samples provided should be such that all the facilities provided in the programme must be tested. For instance if Library Acquisition provides for checking automatically if the invoice amount is more than the price in the order by 15 %, the data in sample bill given for testing should contain at least one bill given for this aspect of Testing. The results you get and the results you ought to get are compared. User involvement is high in this stage.

Programmes are corrected and the process repeated until it is totally error free.

6. Implementation

Implementation of computer based systems may be of three types: (a) Parallel Running, (b) Pilot Running, (c) Overnight change.

(a) Parallel Running : In this method both manual method and computer processing are done simultaneously. Manual method is relied upon for day to day working. Results of computer processing are constantly compared and checked for discrepancies.

It should be borne in mind that errors could be due in existing manual process also! (This may come to light due to high level of accuracy of computerisation). This method is time consuming and the period needed for wholesale switch over can't be easily predicted. Moreover additional temporary hands are needed for checking errors. But this provides a Safe method.

For instance in the case of a book ordering activity, parallel running may be worthwhile as errors in wrong ordering may be expensive.

(b) Pilot Running : In this method two situations are possible. In one case, among the whole target user group, a small section is identified and they are served by Computer System. Rest are served by manual system. This is called Pilot running. All aspects of provisions of the software are tried on the small group of select users.

Alternately, a specified module of the program package may be implemented initially. After gaining confidence, computerisation may be extended using other modules. This is called Phased Implementation.

For example if you have developed a circulation system you may try it out initially with all staff members who are more likely to respond to errors, offer feedback etc.

Again, if you have obtained a software package for all functions of the library activities, you may just wish to implement one of them-Say Acquisition Control-to begin with.

(c) Overnight Change : Obviously this means set a date and start the new system from then on—No manual system is available as parallel or back up facility. Though risks are high, in this method of implementation, there is no money wasted in terms of time, error checking etc. As all persons will be in the same boat, rectification of errors will be speedy.

If you are starting a new service fresh or which is substantially different from earlier service (say SDI), you can straight away opt for this method.

However, each organisation has to weigh the advantages and disadvantages of the above three methods and perhaps use them in combination as well.

7. Running

When the system is up and running there is no much to do except keep-up schedules. You may have to provide for emergencies such as staff on vacation, or sudden leave; power shut downs, computer down time, etc.

8. Review

A fairly running system needs to be reviewed periodically. Reviews will reveal whether we are within the budgets allotted; whether time frames are being adhered to or not. They may even tell us whether the objectives with which computerisation was started have been achieved or not. Results of Review stage will help as input for further computerisation work.

LIBRARY STAFF INVOLVEMENT IN COMPUTERISATION

Right from sate 1 to stage 8 mentioned above the concerned library staff should be actively involved.

In the initial study, it is librarian who identifies repetitive jobs, jobs involving delay etc. In the second stage-specialization of requirements or system analysis–most active involvement is envisaged. Every activity must be observed, explained. Present procedures must be demonstrated and explained. Deviations or exceptions should be spelt out. Librarian must prepare his staff for change. This involved coaxing, understanding, removing fears regarding etc.

Librarian must be involved in Data Validation/error checking stages during design stages. He should also clarify which jobs will be manual and which ones will be computer handled.

The design shown by system Analyst should be fully understood by the Librarian. Librarian should review the contents of the various reports presented during the above stage with respect to:

(a) Terms of reference

(b) Scope of the stage

(c) Recommendations

(d) Plans and time scales

(e) Costs and budgets

(f) Manpower needed etc.

During the program development stage Librarian can get his staff trained for operation, data entry *etc.* He can also plain develop manual procedures to 'fall back' if needed.

During testing stage, Librarian should give valid test data. He should monitor the progress of development in each stage.

New clerical data preparation procedures if any should be explained to staff.

COMPUTER SELECTION AND PURCHASE

The need for buying a computer is initially ascertained through a feasibility study or Systems Analysis. Then depending upon a detailed investigation of *what* is to be computerised, an exhaustive "Requirements Specification" is drawn up. A Computer meeting the requirements thus ascertained is bought and installed.

The selection, purchase and installation of a Computer System may be done in the following stages:

1. Define the Requirements
2. Establish a budget
3. Identify possible suppliers
4. Obtain proposals
5. Evaluate proposals
6. Buy/Install/Test and Use.

1. Define Your Needs

A detailed study of requirements may reveal several things regarding computer needs:

(a) Batch processing vs. Transaction Processing. If batch processing is more predominant, speed may not be a problem; whereas in the case of online enquiry system (Transaction Processing) speed of execution is crucial.

(b) If real time applications are envisaged, the operating system should be capable of handling this aspect.

(c) Volume and Type of reports generated will dictate the type, speed, size of printer, large volume output calls for high speed line or laser printers.

(d) Systems involving large volumes of complicated mathematical computing as in science and engineering areas may need special purpose additional accessories or chips in hardware.

(e) If distributed processing is envisaged linking up systems through LAN may be called for.

2. Establish a Budget

Based on specific requirements, a specific budget must be obtained. This will include all costs computer peripherals consumables, site preparation including wiring, air conditioning, maintenance, initial training, furniture manuals, software etc.

3. Identify Suppliers

Depending upon the organisation's purchase procedure, you may call for proposals, tenders or quotations.

Initial screening of vendors may be done based upon past performance, opinion of other computer installations, vendor rating studies/surveys found in professional journals etc. 4 or 5 vendors may be selected and asked to give proposals.

4. Obtain Proposals

Explain what you want in a general meeting to all vendors. Provide same information to all vendors equally. Offer clarifications to all who ask. Be fair in your approach. Have few more rounds independently with each vendor. Vendor may do his own systems of your needs.

5. Evaluating Proposals

A check list of questions which may be tried to evaluate the vendors is given in the check list appended. Try to get answers to as many questions as possible. You may allot weights for various factors and try to rank the vendors, choose the vendor who ranks first.

6. Buy-Install, Test and Use

The site preparation must have gone ahead in the time we are waiting for the computer to arrive:

(1) We have to decide on the location for computer.

(2) Check flooring–if false, noise free, dust free flooring is needed, this should be done.

(3) Decide Floor Plan of Computer Tape Drives, Card readers peripherals etc.

(4) Provide electrical conduits, fittings and accessories. Voltage stabilizer of required capacity and Air conditioning as needed may be done.

(5) Furniture, Telephone, Office space etc. have to be organised.

(6) Storage space for Floppies, Disks, Tapes, Programme Documentations etc. should be provided.

As soon as computer is installed and system generation is carried out, it should be thoroughly checked and tested for all aspects. Installation is usually done by vendors.

Several Diagnostic tools and software packages are offered. Computer staff should learn the proper use of these tools during installation stage itself.

APPENDIX-I: CHECKLIST FOR EVALUATING A COMPUTER OFFER

A. Manufacturer/Vendor

(1) Is the Manufacturer financially sound?

(2) Do their products, enjoy a good reputation?

(3) What is the installation base of the system proposed to be supplied?

(4) Has the supplier given reference? What do referees say?

(5) Are the supplier's staff knowledgeable and experienced?

(6) Has the supplier approached the task with professionalism?

(7) How fast is the supplier likely to grow? Will he go out of business?

B. Equipment/Hardware

(1) Does it meet the requirements laid down by you?

(2) What is the speed of access in the hard/Floopy Disc?

(3) What is the speed of the printer?

(4) How long does it take to back up?

(5) How much core and auxiliary memory do you get?

(6) What is the speed of execution of instructions?

(7) Can hardware additions be done easily? At what cost?

(8) What is the MTBF?

(9) Does it require any special environment (AC)?

C. Software

(1) What is the operating system?

(2) Latest Version supplied? All standard utilities that should accompany OS supplied? What are the languages offered/supported? What are the version

given? How compatible are they with standard products?

(3) What *application packages* ready made; if any, offered? Has this been demonstrated to your satisfaction? Will each module work as claimed? Does it meet your practical needs? Is it easy to make additions/alternations? Will the vendor support you with later versions? If yes at what cost? How long? Is the software copy protected? Do you have to sign any license agreements? Are there ay run time restrictions? Is the operation straight forward and easy to learn?

(4) How is Data/Record/File Security implemented?

D. The Purchase-After

(1) What is the warranty period?

(2) What items are covered under warranty?

(3) What after sales service is provided?

(4) Is training and initiation help involved?

(5) What is the reputation of supplier/software? Maintenance of hardware? software?

(6) What is the cost of service after sales? Per call basics? Accessories included? Annual contract?

(7) How will supplier handle implementation of Systems? Will he help in site preparation?

(8) What are the ongoing services provided? (a) On the phone help? (b) Flying squad?

(9) Is the vendor committed to the specific product line supplied? Is he thinking of phasing out of it?

E. Miscellaneous Items

(1) Are the manuals for hardware/software etc. useful? Clear? Precise? Accurate?

(2) How much does it cost?

(3) Cost of add-ons? Service Contract? Insurance?

Consumables? Software? Manuals? Installation charges? Taxes? packing? forwarding?

(4) When can the equipment be supplied?

(5) What are payment Terms? Lease? Rental? Instruments? Full advance?

PROGRAMME PACKAGES

Three Types of Software

Software or the programmes that make computers do what we want or needed. They can be grouped under three broad categories: (1) System Software (2) General Purpose software, (3) Specific Application Packages.

System Sqftware

Under the first category we may include such things like Operating Systems, Compilers, Translators, Interpreters, Debuggers, Utilities or Tool kits for enhancing the use of the computer as a whole etc.

General Purpose Software

General purpose software may perhaps consist of Word Processing Software, Spread Sheet Packages, DBMS packages etc. Some popular Word Processing Softwares are: WORDSTAR, WORDLORD, WORDPERFECT etc., VISICALC, SUPERCLAC, LOTUS 123, are spread sheets. Important and popular DBMS packages are dBASE II, dBASE III, dBASE III PLUS, KNOWLEDGEMAN, FOXBASE, RBASE etc.

Application Software

We are primarily interested now in the third category: Specific application packages that are of interest to Librarians.

In a Library the following and similar other major functions may be computerised:

(1) Acquisitions Control

(2) Serials Control
(3) Circulation Control
(4) Information Retrieval
(5) Selective Dissemination of Information
(6) Publishing Abstracting Bulletins
(7) List of Additions
(8) Current Awareness Bulletin.

Total or Piecemeal

We can get total integrated Software Package capable of taking care of most of the functions mentioned above. Or we may buy specific application package say for acquisition control alone.

Bought or Made at Home

Again the application package may be developed within the library or bought from outside. It can also be developed, exclusively for us, by an outside consultancy based upon the detailed specification give by us.

Software Costs

The attitude of software developers in pricing seems to be "Price it at what the market can bear". One can get really sophisticated programs free or for a nominal price or end up paying thousands of rupees for a worthless price of software. A certain amount of gambling and risk can't be eliminated.

SOURCES USED

1. Based on a lecture delivered by Dr. P. Vyasamoorty, Hyderabad.
2. Kumar, P.S.G. *Computerisation of Indian Libraries*, Delhi: BRPC, 1987.

13

Information Networks: Potentialities and Challenges*

WHAT OF NETWORKS

Definition

Network can be defined as a group of individuals or organizations that are interconnected. The advent of computers and new developments in telecommunication technology made networking a global phenomenon. Library and information science institutions are forming networks to achieve better resource sharing and to provide better services to the users.

Aims and Objectives of Library Network

- To promote sharing of resources
- Assist in acquisition and processing of material

* Text of Lecture delivered at the Seminar on Networking and Legislation held at CBRI, Lucknow on 3 Oct, 2002.

- Exchange of documents and data
- Cooperation and coordination in collection development
- Help in the establishment of referral service, online retrieval of information and online union catalogues.
- To build bibliographic databases
- To build various other databases like that of projects, specialists, institutions, etc.
- Electronic mailing,
- File transferring
- Evolve standards and guidelines in techniques, methods, procedures, hardware, software, services and so on.

Uses

Library and Information networks help in

- Online retrieval of bibliographic, numeric, as well as full- text databases;
- Compilation of reading lists, topical bibliographies, etc;
- To have bibliographic control by integrating national library catalogues, etc;
- Automatic book requesting systems;
- Use of CD-ROM products and services;
- Remote data entry facility;
- Downloading of information;
- Library mailing, inter-library requests and lending, etc;
- Document delivery;
- Access to public domine information/data/software; etc.

Prerequisites For Network Organisation

1 Agreements for implementing cooperation
2 Establishment of facilities for sorting little used

materials

3 Agreements on acquisition policies to ensure consistent development of holdings to avoid redundancy

4 Agreements to share the currently owned materials, with protocols, limitations and priorities carefully spelled out

5 Schemes for intelligent organization of data/documents

6 Methods of adequate delivery of resources to users (the output media)

7 The subject interest area should be a common one among the centers being connected

8 Compatibility between the computing systems available with the organizations to be netted is essential

9 To ensure the ability of network among the resource sharing libraries, a compatible record format is highly desirable

10 Standardization of policies and procedures across the network and ad-hered to by all participants in order that these tasks could be performed and shared in efficient manner

11 Adequate means of information dissemination

12 Formal established organizational cooperation

13 Established and functioning communication links (telephone, telex, fax, satellite communication channels)

14 An agreement should exist on acquisition policies to ensure consistent development of holdings and to avoid redundancy

GLOBAL INFORMATION NETWORKS

The evolution of library networks can be traced back to 1901 in which year the Library of Congress started the catalogue card production and distribution service. During the first fifty years of the 20th century the linkage between libraries was mainly for inter-library loan, bibliographic control and quality catalogue card service. But, with the use of computers from the early 1960s the concept, scope and use of network has totally changed.

The year 1965 heralded a new era in communication with the orbiting of 'Early Bird' telecommunication satellite by the United States. Geostationary satellites made it easy and fast to communicate across the globe.

The marriage between computer and communication technology resulted in new discipline called "compunications" which made it easy to pass images; as well as, documents alongwith voice. Communication satellites marked the end of isolation.

Online library networks can be categorized by the type of service they provide into two:

1 **Search Services :** Provide multiple databases for online searching; and

2 **Customised Service Networks :** Offer graphic and other files which users can search and modify even for their own use.

GROUPING OF NETWORKS

Networks can be generally grouped into open networks and closed networks. An open network is public and is available to virtually anyone. The telephone system is a good example of this type. In a closed network, only users who have a direct, close relationship to the application have connections.

Network Topologies

"Topology" is a mathematical term which refers to the way the interconnection paths between the many users, or nodes are arranged. There are many ways to run channels that allow data to go from one user node to another user node. The simplest way is to have a path from each user of the network to every other. Star topology, Bus topology, Ring topology etc are the important types of topologies used in different network systems.

COMPUTER- COMMUNICATION NETWORKS

The interweaving of computing and communication had led to information networks of great complexity and utility. Transmission lines can be used to connect a computer to another computer or a computer terminal to another computer. However, point-to-point connections do not provide the flexibility. Networks of lines can have following prominent features such as,

(i) Multiple connection

Connecting a computer or terminal to any of a number of other computers at various location.

(ii) Sharing

Permitting several terminals or computers to use the same transmission line alternately.

(iii) Multiplexing

Permitting several terminals or computers to translate data over the same transmission line simultaneously.

(iv) Message Packing

Interleaving data into the line so that idle periods of one transmitter can be used to send data from another.

INDIAN NETWORKS

General

Sr. No.	Network	Setting Up body	Service & Functioning
1	NICNET	National Informatics Centre, Planning Commission, New Delhi	Provides computing and communication infrastructure to aid planning & monitoring, decision making activities, facilitates flow of Info among 32 state and 439 district nodes, Evolved as a MIS to cater the needs of Govt. Depts and agencies.
2.	INDONET	CMC Limited, Hyderabad	Commercial computer network, designed for intracity communication. It operates in a star network with control point at Delhi, using packet switching technology.

NICNET

NICNET was developed by the National Informatics Centre (NIC), Planning Commission, Government of India in 1972. The primary objective of the network is to provide computing and communicating infrastructure aid to planning and monitoring of schemes and decision making activities in the government. The first phase of this network comprised of intra-city network in Delhi connecting interactive terminals and computers with a Cyber 170/730 system. The facilities that such a network could offer was demonstrated during Asian Games (1982); and Non-Aligned Meet (NAM) (1984). It has regional centers in Pune, Hyderabad and Bhubaneshwar.

Under this network all state capitals and district headquarters are linked together. The network applied spread spectrum multiple access technique and C-200 series micro earth stations installed in all state and district centers. The network facilitates flow of information among the four regional nodes (including Delhi); 32 State/union Territory nodes and 439 district nodes.

A number of information systems have been established under NICNET which include Accounts, Budget, Loans, Plan monitoring, Customs, Central-Excise, Import/Export data, Estate duty,- Economics, Socio-economic Indicators, Media, Water and Irrigation, Rural Development, Mines and Minerals, Forestry and Wild Life, Small-scale Industries, Tourism, Energy, Health, Census, Education, Manpower and Management.

INDONET

INDONET is the first commercial computer network evolved by the Computer Maintenance Corporation (CMC) Ltd., Hyderabad. In the first phase, the network consisted of installing three IBM 4361 computers, at Calcutta, Mumbai and Chennai; PDP 11/44 at Delhi; and ROB 1055 at Hyderabad with access points in the cities of Bangalore, Ahmedabad and Pune. It has adopted IBM's System Network Architecture and uses dedicated lines of 2400/4800 bps.

In the second phase the number was to increase to 100. It operates as a STAR network with control point at Delhi using rooftop 3 pm earth stations and packet-switching technology for routing of data from central station to other INDONET centers.

INDONET has been connected to the international gateway of Videsh Sanchar Nigam Ltd (VSNL), Mumbai thereby facilitating entry in public data networks of other countries. It has been planned as a geographically dispersed computer network linking scattered organizations in India. It helps in the export of software. It has a distributed data processing system and can process large amount of scientific and industrial data. It also helps to promote key computer related technologies like databases, management programming techniques, computer graphics and the like; and provide connectivity to GTE-Telnet and TYMNET computer networks of USA; DATEX-P of Germany; TRANSPAC of France, etc.

Switching nodes and 12 remote access points with its Network Management Centre at Delhi. While nodes in the four cities namely Kolkata, Mumbai, Delhi and Chennai, will meet at 64,000 bps, the other nodes and access points were connected at 9,600 bps.

Network Development Efforts By Other Public Agencies

INET	Department of Telecommunications	Available in 89 cities in phase II
Integrated Services Digital Network	Department of Telecommunications	Now available in 60 cities for audio image and data communication
Remote Area Business Network (RABMN)	Department of Telecommunications	Only for organizations in remote areas. Subscription now closed.
Gateway Packet Switching	Videsh Sanchar Nigam Ltd, (VSNL) and local PADs in 10 major cities for international linkage	Gateway system in Bombay

ONLINE NATIONAL ACCESS CENTRES TO INTERNATIONAL DATABASE SERVICES

Sr. No.	City	Host institute
1	Bengaluru	National Aeronautical Laboratory (NAL)
2	Kolkata	Association for Cultivation of Science (IACS)
3	Chennai	Central Leather Research Institute (CLRI)
4	New Delhi	Indian National Scientific Documentation Centre (INSDOC)
5	Pune	National Chemical laboratory (NCL)

National Access centers to international database services use international carriers via Gateway Packet Switching Services (GPSS) at Mumbai.

Sr. No.	Network	Setting up body	Service & Functioning
1.	BTISNET Biotechnology Information System Network	Department of Biotechnology, Govt of India, New Delhi	9 DISCS, DBTAPEX body, 23 DISCS, to facilitate the access to user centers identified at educational and R & D institutions. BTTS has been established to serve as a database management organization in six identified areas involving two specialized centers connected by micro earth stations.
2.	CSIR NET	Council of Scientific & Industrial Research, DSIR, Govt of India, New Delhi	40 and odd laboratories are connected by computer communication network. Apart from accessing international databases, through NACID's indigenous online database, provides access to different subjects like leather technology, food technology, natural products, chemistry, radio physics and medicinal plants
3	DESNET	DESIDOC New Delhi	Bibliographic and Information network for defence covering unclassified and technical information.
4	ERNET	Joint venture of research organisations	Computer network for academic and research community with 8 leading

			institutions like IIT's Indian Institute of Science, and National Centre for Software Technology 2 institutions of DOE. Its Electronic Mail, file transfer, remote log-on, database access, and bulletin board.
5.	VIDYANET	Joint venture for academic and research organisations	A network of 10 institutions. Aims at providing day-to-day research information. Scope for linkage with EARN, Geneva and BITNET.

BTISNET

The Department of Biotechnology, Government of India has set up ten specialized information centers in genetic engineering, cell culture and virology, plant tissue culture, photosynthesis and plant molecular biology, oncogenes, reproduction physiology, cell transformation nucleic acid and protein sequences, immunology and bioprocess engineering. 23 user centers have been identified and the entire system is piggyback on NICNET to take advantage of its communication facilities and computing power.

SIRNET

SIRNET (= Scientific and Industrial Research Network) is a computer and communication network for CSIR laboratories, SIRNET has one mail node called CSIRD (in Delhi) and several user nodes, SIRNET is located at INSDOC, New Delhi. It is connected to ERNET set-up by the DOE with financial assistance from UNDP, EARNET inturn is connected to UUNET (= Unix User Network) through which other international networks like BITNET, CSNET and JANET are accessible. These networks together span all major countries like USA, Canada, UK and other European countries, Australia and Japan.

DESINET

DESINET is a bibliographic information network for Defence covering only unclassified scientific and technical information. This network has close links with other similar networks like NICNET for exchange of information on mutually agree terms.

ERNET

ERNET (= Education and Research Network) is a computer network for academic and research community in India, Starting with eight leading institutions the IITs; Indian Institute of Science, Bangalore; National Centre for Software Technology (NCST), Mumbai and Department of Electronics (DOE). It aims at linking hundreds of academic and research institutions covering a number of scientific and engineering disciplines. It has started setting up campus-wide networks (LANs) and a backbone of satellite based Wide Area Networks (WANs) are being implemented.

VIDYANET

VIDYANET aims at connecting scientists and research workers in the laboratories/ institutions of excellence in the country. The first phase was to rover All India Institute of medical Science (AIIMS), New Delhi; Indian Agricultural Research Institute (IARI), New Delhi; IITs; Indian Statistical Institute (ISI), Kolkata; Bhabha Atomic Research Centre (BARC), Mumbai; Institute of Geomagnetism, Hyderabad; National Centre for Software Technology (NCST), Mumbai; and Tata Institute of Fundamental Research (TIFR), Mumbai. In subsequent phases it is envisaged to connect major institutions in Ahmedabad, Bengaluru, Bhopal, Kolkata and Chennai.

The major objective of VIDYANET is to stimulate cooperative research, day-to-day exchange of research information and the execution of joint projects and publications. It also intends to allow users to develop databases on specialized areas.

SPECIALISED NETWORKS

RAILNET (Network of Indian Railways); COALNET (Network of Coal India Ltd.); SAILNET (Steel Authority of India Ltd. Network); BANKNET (National Network of Banks) are in progress.

LIBRARY NETWORKS

INFLIBNET

The Information and Library Network (INFLIBNET) programme was initiated by the University Grants Commission (UGC) in April 1991. It aims at linking libraries and information centers, institutions of national importance, R & D institutions, etc thereby improving the capability in information handling and services. It is a cooperative venture for pooling, sharing and optimization of library resources in the country.

Metropolitan Area Networks

Name of Library Network	Year of starting	Promoting agency	Whether registered as a society	No. of participating libraries	Database development & other activities
ADINET	1993	Soc.	Yes INFLIBNET & NISSAT	9	Library holdings database in progress. Library automation in progress. Training programmes Database of current periodicals in member libraries.
BALNET	1995	NISSAT	Yes		Activities will start after getting financial support from NISSAT.

BONET	1994	NCST & NISSAT	No		Online union catalogue of periodicals. Online request system for ILL. E-mail & Internet access. Online searching of foreign databases. Data base on computers and software. CD-ROM database searching, Database of contents of Indian periodicals. Software for OPAC.
CALIB-NET	1992	NISSAT	Yes	10	Library automation in progress. Access to Internet and Knight-Ridder (Dialog). CD-ROM database searching.
DELNET	1990	Soc, NIC & NISSAT	Yes	54	Books database (1.68 lakh records). Multilingual books database. E-mail service. Union list of current periodicals (11,000 records). Data-base of Indian specialists. Online searching of foreign databases.
MALIB NET	1993	Soc, INSDOC	Yes	15	Current serials database of 50 libraries. Journal holdings database (15 member libraries, 500 journals). Journal contents database (10,000 records from member libraries). All INSDOC databases ported on MALIBNET (10 DATABASES). Online Searching of these databases. Automotive engineering

					database (4,500 records). Access to Internet and Knight-Ridder. (Dialog) database. CD-ROM database searching
MYLIB-NET	1994	Soc, Mysore Library Consortium & NISSAT	Yes	9	Library automation in progress

CALIBNET

NISSAT took the initiative for the design and development of metropolitan library networks since 1985. Calcutta Library Network (CALIBNET) is the first one in this direction. CALIBNET was inaugurated in 1993. In 1994 CALIBNET Society was formed which functions as a coordinating agency for the network.

CALIBNET serves the collective interest of Calcutta's institutional libraries by means of computer-based library automation and networking aimed at optimum utilization of bibliographic resources of these libraries by a mechanism of resource sharing and electronic access. The prime objective is to institute systematic inter-library cooperation and document delivery amongst the libraries of Calcutta. Thereby, they can stimulate resource sharing.

DELNET

The Delhi Library Network (DELNET) is the first operational library network in India sponsored by NISSAT and started as a project of the India International Centre in 1988. It was registered as a Society in June 1992. However, the same network is now designated as Developing Library Network.

The main objectives of DELNET are to promote sharing of resources among the libraries by developing a network; storing and dissemination of information; offering computerized information service to users; and to coordinate efforts of suitable collection development and reducing unnecessary duplication wherever possible.

Other Networks

BONET

BONET (Bombay Library Network) was started in 1994 as a joint project of NCST, Bombay and NISSAT of DSIR, New Delhi. It has created a database of 15,000 items on computers and software technology. It has a union catalogue of journals and other periodicals in 10 libraries in the region. A number of CD-ROM databases are available on a Novell server and are accessible over a Local Area Network. Software has been created for online catalogue. In addition BONET hosts a database of tables of contents of Indian periodicals created by the National Centre for Information, Mumbai.

MALIBNET

MALIBNET (= Madras Library Network) was registered as a society in February 1993 and the network become operational in June 1993. INSDOC is the executive agency for the MALIBNET project. There are 10 institutional members and 5 associate institutional members. At present 4 databases : (i) Current Serials; (ii) Contents database of current journals; (iii) Holdings database; and (iv) Automotive engineering database are being maintained. Services of MALIBNET includes E-Mail connectivity to all members; MALIBNET card (for users to have access to the resources of libraries of MALIBNET), Contents, Abstracts and Photocopy Services (CAPS); Express document procurement and delivery.

ADINET

ADINET (= Ahmedabad Library Network) was inaugurated formally in February 1995. This is the fifth library network sponsored by NISSAT. It has created (i)

Institute Master (a database of 74 libraries in Ahmedabad); (ii) Journal Master (Serial/journal database currently subscribed by member libraries); and (iii) Book Master (Union Catalogue of books). Services of ADINET includes online information search; Inter Library loan; photocopying service from various databases; E-Mail service and Bulletin-board service.

OTHERS

Those in the offering are:

BALNET (= Bangalore Library Network); MYLIBNET (= Mysore Library Network); PUNET (= Pune Library Network); HYLIBNET (= Hyderabad Library Network) are at various stages in operation.

Problems with Library Network in India

Most of the General networks are playing a little role in communicating scientific and technical information. Their objectives and functions are different. Most of the national access centres mentioned above are defunct. Many of the metropolitan Area Networks are in existence only for name sake, except with the exception of DELNET and to some extent CALIBNET.

Major reason for the failure of these systems is lack of finance and no much participation by the libraries.

The Internet

Vulnerability of Networks

The Internet, during a very short period, has been adapted for various commercial applications, which brought a paradigm shift in the way business being conducted across the globe. The Internet access has increased the speed and efficiency of business-to-business (B2B) and business-to-consumer (B2C) processes to unimagined levels. The computer connectivity that provide a basis for information sharing can also be a conduit for access and leakage of the confidential information to unauthorized persons, intentionally or unintentionally. Ensuring internet security is, therefore, becoming an essential tool for handling business activities in the twenty-first century. It is not only the external interference, even the employees of an organization may expose their networked computers to dangerous viruses or other malicious or harmful codes by accessing or downloading files of unknown origin. And, unlike earlier viruses, which were designed to infect single computers, the latest generations of viruses have been specifically designed for the computer networks and the World Wide Web. Viruses, such as Melissa, Explore, zip, and love letter have clearly demonstrated their potential threats by spreading through the entire networks within a few minutes. The organization will have to implement a comprehensive Internet security programmes to protect themselves from these threats.

As of today, the Internet connects an estimated 30 million computers in 195 countries including Antarctica. The strength of the Internet in reaching millions of people world over is also its weakness. The users may believe that their site will not be a target or that they have taken sufficient precautions. Because the technology is constantly changing and, intruders are constantly developing new tools and techniques, no solution shall remain effective indefinitely.

During May 2001, anonymous web site attacks forced Yahoo, which receives 8.74 million visitors a day, to remain shut for 5 hours. Ebay, which receives 1.68 million visitors a day also crashed for 5 hours. Other targets included ZDNet, which has 734,000 visitors a day, crashed for 3.75 hours. Buy-com, which has 122,000 visitors a day, crashed for 6 hours, Amazon Which has 892,000 visitors a day crashed for 3.75 hours and E trade which has 183,000 visitors a day, crashed for 2.75 hours. According to the Yankee Group, an Internet market research firm, these attacks could cost the victims $1.2 billion in revenues.

An anonymous corporate spy could send an innocent looking e-mail or promise a free version of any popular commercial software programme to an employee of the organization, who has access to the computer that communication may contain a secret Trojan horse programme that creates a backdoor entry into the target computer. The proprietary information and access to the network then gets exposed to the eavesdropper. The electronic bugging device of the 21" century does not use batteries or have an antenna. One does not need to change the tapes. Cursory inspections of backer/cracker sites reveal that many of these digital spy tools are readily available for downloading them hundreds of Internet web sites. The message therefore is simple. It is time to be enlightened. There is no such thing as true computer and network security. Computer based proprietary information is vulnerable to loss and theft.

The Net of today may be a trap tomorrow. Be prepared to face the problems boldly. Future attacks may not be on 'twin towers' but on information networks to make nations weak and vulnerable.

14

Electronic Journals : Consortia Approach*

ELECTRONIC JOURNALS-BENEFITS AND LIMITATIONS

The advantages of electronic journals can be summerised as :

(a) Electronic journals allow for more in the scientific communication process.

(b) It is possible to add experimental data, software and even multimedia extensions.

(c) Electronic journals demand neither library space nor shelving costs nor can they be stolen from library.

(d) Electronic journals are available 24 hours a day, 7 days a week.

(e) Articles can be linked with the body of scholarly literature.

---

* Keynote Address delivered at the National Workshop on "College Libraries' Automation" held at Kamla Nehru College, Korba (Chhattisgarh) on 6 Nov., 2009.

(f) There is a provision for a more open peer review process.

(g) The cost of the electronic journal is likely to be less than its print version in future depending on the availability of both the versions.

Costs

The cost of electronic journals is speculated upon and it is still unsettled whether it will be less expensive than print journals (Friend, 2000). This important point has been the base for the formation of consortia, to share the cost of the access fee to the expensive electronic journals. A more fundamental problem raised by Meets and Gierman(1991) is that the electronic journal could become parallel to the printed journal and thereby and extra burden, not alleviating but aggravating the serials price crisis. As Joyce (1997) mentions the costs of electronic journals are inflated because the publishers have added the cost of producing the standard paper to the cost of adding on the electronic features to produce the electronic version.

Character and Limitations

Libraries are always concerned and more interested in copyright issue. Librarians have the dual role to project the publishers as well the users interest. They undertake the responsibility of making the users aware of their role in : Fair use of the electronic access to the journals. Davis and Reentry (1998) believe that the licensing of electronic journals requires legal expertise and skills beyond the training and experience of most librarians.

ELECTRONIC JOURNALS – INDIAN SCENARIO

In India, many research libraries and some university libraries are already accessing the electronic counterpart of the printed journals, which they are subscribing to. Most of these journals have the online access free along with the print subscription. For the last two or three years, many publishers and vendors were experimenting with their different pricing strategies to the libraries in India. Some of them started the offer to online access to the electronic journals free on a trial basis, wherever the libraries were subscribing to their print versions. As a next step, a few publishers offered their electronic journals for a nominal fee in addition to the print journals. The publishers were trying to arrive at a price, suitable to the libraries, especially for those in the developing countries (Louts, et al. 2001).

While the libraries in North America and Europe were accessing the online journals, the libraries in India were still struggling to set up the infrastructure required for online access to journals. As a result there is delay in acquiring the electronic journals and databases in Indian libraries. Additionally, our library budgets do not give the flexibility to buy the much-required high-tech format of the information. Librarians are in a fix, as to how to manage accessing information within their budget. In addition, they are also expected to bargain for accessing more information. This is precisely what libraries in other countries have managed by establishing some formal networks like consortia, which have the ability to bargain collectively with the commercial-publishers. The same concept or the trend has spared to our country in recent times. More and more publisher have shown interest and willingness to have a dealing with librarians in india. They expect the librarians to have a formal commitment among themselves before they start bargaining with the publishers. In the absence of standardized formal consortia arrangements within the country, it is a difficult situation for India libraries to accept the existing procedure for consortia models in other countries. The objective of this study is to establish some guidelines for the formation of consortia among Indian libraries capacity to administer the electronic journals in science and technology disciplines.

CONSORTIA APPROACH

Consortia are nothing but cooperative efforts which manages all the library service collectively. If has the purpose of exploring the need collectively. This partnership fosters pride, determination and a sense of ownership between its constituent libraries and staff. Consortia are regarded as an effective strategy to increase the buying power of individual libraries over the short term and as an opportunity maximize the efforts of cooperative collection building for resource sharing over the long term (Richer, 1999). It is essential to understand the definition of the term "consortium" which is a powerful cooperative strategy.

The following definitions from the available sources are the derivation from the basic term of "Consortium."

A consortium is said to be " a cooperative arrangement among groups or institutions, or an association or society" (American Heritage Dictionary)

Consortia In India

Libraries are taking the consortia to which they belong a great deal more seriously, than was the case a few years back. They offer libraries the ability to give users the access they are coming to expect and demand to a much broader range of materials than any one library could possibly offer.

Managing library funds judiciously so as to access maximum information is the situation in any library. Hence, this aspect needs serious thought especially in the Indian libraries which are now in the process of utilizing the potential of information technology in library activities. Many libraries especially research libraries in India have their own networks existing in their own geographical areas (Harass, 1993).

By some estimates, today worldwide there are nearly 250 consortia. The most useful experience is not to classify but to understand the key factors of objectives that affect why and how consortia are built and managed. The same principle is applied in designing a suitable model, exploiting the common objectives to take care of most of the requirements (Wade, 1999).

No two consortia are identical. Some are highly structured, while some are loose federations. Some enjoy substantial funding, while others exist in very unfavorable economic conditions. Some have a long history, and others are very young. They also have strong membership support, with a clear agenda and commitment to that agent from member institutions (Helmer, 1999)

The need for an Indian national consortium of libraries to share the access to and cost of the electronic journals has often been discussed in many forums, since there is no common base for many of the libraries, which would benefit from the consortium membership, the concept of a widely agreed consortium has not materialized in India so far. The few consortia which have sprung up in the last two years have managed to take off and also sustain until now, due to different reasons.

INDIAN CONSORTIA

FORSA (Model 1 : Forum for Resource Sharing in Astronomy)

Indian Astrophysics consortium grew out of the efforts of a handful of librarians from institutions specialize in Astrology and Astrophysics in India. This consortium also known as FORSA consisting of 5 members (From the initial & members only 5 joined the consortium for negotiating licensing for Astronomy journals) identified a subscription agent as a supplier of journals. Subscriptions for both paper and electronic format are paid through the supplier. The whole negotiation is based on the number of print journals and hence the sales volume dictates the prices paid for the titles. The more the number of titles the less the price paid decreasing by a few percentage points. This supplier has agreed to be a negotiator between the member and the publisher to provide access to the licensed materials. The concept of establishing a consortium of this kind was born out of the necessity to access the most expensive titles in astronomy published by the particular publisher (Bridle 2002).

The salient features of FORSA consortium are :

Members of the consortium belong to institutes specializing in Astronomy and Astrophysics.

The journal titles for which the consortium license is negotiated are subject focused.

Since the number of members constituting this consortium is small, there is an added advantage for a better communication and understanding between the members and between the agent/publisher.

The publishers find it convenient to negotiate with the members through the agent since the individual invoicing is raised by the agent to the individual members.

The model is worked out for cross e-sources to the print journals subscribed by the members of the consortium and hence equal access for all the members.

No additional requirement of budget for the members in terms of subscription to new print journals since they already subscribed titles to be maintained (Subject to the normal increase in subscription).

Saving on the additional fee for electronic access, which is more for those who do not belong to the consortium.

The most important feature is that the members are not burdened with peripheral.

INDEST (Indian Digital Library in Engineering Science and Technology)

The Indian Digital liberty in Engineering Science and

Technology (INDEST) consortium is an initiative from the Ministry of Human Resource Development (MHRD) of Government of India setup in Dec. 2002. This consortium has been planned to have a "Consortia - based subscription to Electronic Resources for Technical Education in India it has many objectives with reference to the selection of its members and also the electronic products to which they have consortia licensing. The majority of the members of this consortium belong to the IISc and NITs. They all have the common funding agency as part of the MHRD.

The electronic resources proposed for the consortia are based on the following criteria : (Arora, 2002)

1. Well established mule-disciplinary resources with broad coverage were preferred over highly specialized sources targeted for specialists.
2. The electronic resources already on subscription in the beneficiary institutions were preferred over those, which are not being used in any of the beneficiary institutions;
3. Resources that are "electronic only" were preferred over those that are print based unless completely unavoidable;
4. Resources that are very important but highly cost intensive were preferred over those which are less important or less -used but low cost:
5. Resources where electronic versions are made available free on subscription to their print versions were avoided as for as possible; and
6. The INDEST came into existence in Dec. 2002 through its head quarter at the IIT, Delhi. This consortium would directly, or indirectly benefit most of the engineering and technical institutions in India.

Indian Institute of Management Libraries Consortia Model

Need of resource sharing was realized by IIM (Indian

Institutes of Management) Libraries long back, Besides entering into the interlibrary loan, IIM libraries also thought of resources sharing in many other areas such as cooperative processing and decentralized utilization. Two areas were identitied for IIM consortium (i.e.) Developing the collection on shared basis and developing the services for exploiting such collection through IIM Library consortium has in the last one year successfully executed a few shared acquisition services viz. Science Direct of Elsevier, John Wiley electronic journals, and Kluwer electronic journals. Most of the services are identified for partnership.

Members of IIM Consortium

The following members were there in the IIM Library consortium:

a. Indian Institute of Management, Ahmedabad
b. Indian Institute of Management, Bengaluru
c. Indian institute of Management, Kolkata
d. Indian Institute of Management, Indore
e. Indian Institute of Management, Kozhikode
f. Indian Institute of Management, Lucknow

The librarians of all the IIMs have been interacting extensively in the recent past on the possible resource sharing of the CD-ROM/Digital Databases being regularly subscribed to by them. The objective is toward the optimum utilisation and enhancement of the resources, and towards minimizing the expenditure, by consortia based subscriptions to the commonly subscribed databases.

Future Plan

It is envisaged to have an IIM Digital library based on Internet technology to provide the IIM community (Faculty and students) an online web enabled access to the information resources available in all the IIMs without any barriers of time and distance. It will be a simple, efficient and cost effective system. The basic operating principle of this system is decentralized processing and centralized utilization of the literature survey and also the recent discussion and presentations by the IIM Iberians, during the Round Table on Consortia Models, it is realized that this library consortia model is working well for the second year also (Chikkamallaiah, 2002) since this model has homogenous members (six IIM libraries with same status) it does not have any clash with their mutual interests discipline wise, and also all the members share the additional cost equally towards the access fee.

IGCAR Experience with Science Direct

IGCAR (Indira Gandhi Center for Atomic Research), at Kalpakkam operates under the Department of Atomic Energy, Government of India, and has 12 units and 14 field stations all over India. They are of the earlier group of libraries in India to bargain with Elsevier, for access to *Science Direct* for all their members. They have a commitment to maintain their present print subscription for the next three years. Elsevier has committed their prinking for e-access as 9% of the print subscription with a 5% cap on the print subscription ever year.

They have derived the following benefits :

1. All the member institute are able to access science Direct online consisting of 1700 journals, with the access to back files from 1995.
2. They have access to more than 65% of non-subscribed journals.
3. Access to *Science Direct* is enabled *via* IP authorization and password.
4. Access is available to all the units and field stations.
5. Additional access to Bio Med. Net -Full text trends and current opinion.

6. Access to Cell press Online.
7. Since all the members belonging to this consortium are under one parent organization, namely the Department of Atomic energy, They have the advantage of funding from a central agency. Moreover, the administrative procedure required for the initiation of a consortium and its maintenance is taken care of a central unit in IGCAR. They have this required infrastructure, by way library networks and organizational network (Intranet) high need Internet connectivity and the most important requisite of trained manpower to successfully operate a consortium.

UGC and INFLIBNET Initiative of the University System (INFONET)

Though the focus of this study is towards science and Technology libraries in India, one of the consortia models established for the university system in India is discussed here, which has successfully initiated a model for resources subscriptions for their members.

There are 297 universities in Indian, out of which 150 are assisted by UGC (University Grants Commission) and 142 universities are funded by INFLIBNET.

The initiative of e-resources subscription from UGC and INFLIBNET in the 10th five year plan is to provide wider and larger access to electronic journals and data bases. The basic current journals collection has an average of 250 titles. Out of which 60% are Indian publications, as a few universities do not subscribe to any foreign journals. A model which is being proposed to satisfy their member libraries include the following points.

1. This model will provide access to and support only electronic version.

2. It is decide not to link this model with print subscription.
3. This mode! will enable perpetual access to subscribed resources, and archival access for back issues.
4. This model to include few print subscriptions.
5. The subscription to journals commitment for minimum 3 years initially.
6. This commitment to be reviewed at the end of three years.

Methodology

The implementation of this project is worked out in a phased manner:

A. To group the universities according to four subjects as focus; i.e. the resources being journals and bibliographic databases.
B. Major funding (up to 90%) is from UGC towards the implementation of this project.
C. Technically and administratively, INFLIBNET will administer, maintain and monitor the project in different stages.
D. Selection of the focus discipline and the potential resources will be identified through experts from universities.
E. The participating universities will sign a MOU with UGC and INFLIBNET since, both these bodies are responsible for the implementation of this project, by way of funding and technical support.
F. Initiate the project with a pilot attempt in select disciplines.

The major issues involved in implementing projects of this nature are:

(a) Identification of universities (as members of the consortium) to be served.

(b) Identification of resources (Journals and databases) to be provided through the consortium deal to its members:

(c) The very important issue of identification of potential publishers and vendors or aggregators who will be partners in this project.

(d) To start the pilot work, the four disciplines focused are identified as (a) Biological science (b) Chemistry (c) Mathematics and (d) Physics, Currently an expert group has been formed in August 2002, which has initiated this interaction with 142 universities who have shown interest in this project These universities are identified to join the consortium based on the following criteria:

1. Departments specializing in selected four disciplines
2. Number of faculty members
3. students
4. Number of pH Ds
5. NAAC Accreditation
6. Network infrastructure
7. Research contribution in terms of publications

The same expert group with the assistance from the universities will the assistance from the universities will identify the resources to be shared among the members. The major task of identifying the publishers belonging to either commercial or non-profit making associations will also be undertaken after the discussion with major publishers/ aggregators and others (Kumbar 2002.)

Future Plan

It is expected to extend this initiative to other areas, including humanities and social sciences. It is envisaged to include more universities, depending on the active participation and cooperation received from them. The essential issue of support of funding is required from the government and UGC on long-terms basis.

This model is in its initial place of conducting the pilot work for identification of members and resources. If it can be implemented and monitored successfully, it will be a major consortium model with more members and resources in the university system in India.

Consortium - CSIR Experience

The Council of Scientific and Industrial Research (CSIR) established in 1942 is India's largest research and development organization. It has 40 Laboratories spread over the country. The council is responsible for research and development in science and technology.

The major objective of CSIR consortia is to strengthen CSIR library resources by pooling sharing and providing electronic access to scholars and scientists of CSIR labs and to promote the culture of electronic access in their libraries.

The initiation of the consortium process started with a meeting of" enterprising" librarians at NCL, Pune in April 2000. This meeting was followed up with the " CSIR librarians meet" in Feb. 2001 at Regional Laboratory at Trivandrum.

Methodology

The first proposal on consortium was submitted to the Director General of CSIR in March 2001. Around the same time, Elsivior had opened up their extensive trial for *Science Direct* to the members of CSIR libraries.

A study group was set-up, in May 2001, and a report was prepared and submitted in October 2001. In Dec. 2001, a Negotiations Committee was set up to go into details of the access to *Science Direct*. This committee met again in Jan. 2002, to discuss more about this project.

ICICI Knowledge Park: JCCC@ Virtual Information Center

The VIC (Virtual Information Center) is a NISSAT funded project, committed for three years. JCCC@ VIC is a consortium effort to mobilize electronic Journal resources.

This is a typical example of group of libraries, accessing electronic journals, facilities by an aggregator in India. It is called JCCC J-gate custom content for consortia. The following are the features of JCCC:

1. It provides the customized private portal for accessing the journals " Subscribed by the consortia.
2. It also gives Intranet solution for seamless access to subscribed e-Journals. Similar to the direct subscription to the publishers and vendors subscription through aggregators also supports automatic password Authentication.
3. Links are visible only for journals to which online access rights are accrued by the accessing harbor
4. JCCC is a virtual library model for accessing and sharing available print journal resources.

Objective

Union list of Electronic journals of participating member libraries. Databases of list of articles published in these journals. A search mechanism to locate articles by simple search.

Facility to peruse abstract and move on to full text (pd. or htm, etc.) on publisher's Web site in a seamless fashion. Facility to ask for a copy of the paper from local librarian or to get it from a participating member library.

Facility for customizing users requirements of certain specific titles via " May TOC" feature.

Members of JCCC @ VIC

VIC consortium consists of Members belonging to:

Virtual Information Center

University of Hyderabad

National Institute of Nutrition

National Chemical Laboratory,

ICRISAT

Center for Cellular and Molecular Biology,

Initially, the purpose of forming the consortium was not so much as to subscribe to journals, but chiefly to optimize the use of electronic journal resources. It started its operation from July 2002.

Methodology

The important aspect of the formal agreement among the members is taken care of in this consortium arrangement by the participating members and facilitator, Virtual Information Center (VIC).

VIC is the facilitator for the members and its entered into an agreement with service provider and placed an order. The service provider in turn, created databases and hosted them on a central web server with suitable search and fetch mechanism. As far participating members, they managed to complete certain administrative routines to managed to complete certain administrative routines to enable seamless 'linkages to publisher's to publisher's Webster for access to full text articles. To complete the cycle the end users in participating organizations use the facility their desktops by using the simple web browser, place inter-library loan requests, search TOC database etc.

SNDT/LISA (Library and Information Science Abstracts Consortium)

In this arrangement, SNDT University in Mumbai has taken the lead to negotiation, which benefits the universities to access LISA on web as well as the CD. The principal model offered to the members is calculated on the number of users, with a pre-determined condition on the minimum number of members to be 5 to align the agreement. Though the list price is Sterling Pound 1000/- The members have the facility of accessing the LISA in print on 20% discount, and the web access is freely attached to the print (Govern, 2002).

Compared to other consortia arrangements, this consortium has a leader who has taken the initiative to negotiate the product on behalf of other members. But the actual sense of leading a joint effort is not visible. The members have approached an agent to be their negotiator with the publisher.

The pre-determined condition of specifying the minimum number of members will be a problem since at a later stage the consortium will not have smooth functioning if any of the member drops out. Moreover this pricing model calculated on the number of users, is offered to the universities outside India, and the same cannot be applied to the universities in India.

CONCLUSION

Thus, inclusion of other libraries into the consortia will have access to large number of electronic journals at a very low payment. Electronic journals are definitely more advantageous when compared with print versions.

Continuous access to the journals need funds, institutional support and continuous policy with regard to supply and access.

REFERENCE

1. Kumar, PSG, Fundamentals of Information Science ED3 . Delhi : Indraprastha : 2008.

TYPES OF LIBRARIES

Public

15

Public Library Services: Past, Present and Future*

LIBRARY MOVEMENT

Before independence there were many reasons for a sound library movement in India. Most of the people were illiterate and were being exploited by the government as well as by the fellow human beings. They needed a lot of information for improving their standard of living and save themselves from exploitation by the rich and lay leaders.

Library movement was regarded before independence as a powerful means to enlighten the common man with information needed for protection from exploitation, improve their health and increase their standard of living.

Before 1910 libraries were few and were mean for chosen few. The free public library movement owes its origin to the visionary ruler of Baroda Maharaja Sayajirao Gaekwad

* Paper presented at the National Conference on "Public Libraries in the Knowledge Societies" organised by A P Library Association from 9-11 July 2010 at Hyderabad.

exactly a century ago. He not only established public libraries but also tried to organise them on scientific lines. Soon after, other princely states also followed suite the example of Baroda State.

In Andhra Pradesh on contrary to Baroda, the library movement was described aptly as the "peoples' movement". It was learned men who took lead in the establishment of a library association and through this organization tried to establish public libraries throughout the state and organize them on scientific lines by training library workers in the art and craft of librarianship.

In some other states and regions people took it as an essential requisite for a town to have a library and see that people use them for their own benefit. Some of these libraries served as shelters for housing manuscripts and other rare and valuable ones. The Mitra Mandal Libraries; Gokhale Libraries; and Native General Libraries are some such examples.

During British regime, government supported national level institutions of scientific, academic and public libraries.

After Independence

After independence creation of CSIR, UGC, ICAR, ICMR etc. started taking care of research and academic libraries, Particularly university and college libraries.

Special assistance was being provided under different plan periods for establishment and development of public libraries. Assistance was provided to different states for the establishment/strengthening of State central libraries, district libraries, mobile library services, etc.

Public Libraries and RRRLF

Establishment of Raja Rammohun Roy Library Foundation in 1972 is a land-mark development for public libraries in India.

STATE OF PUBLIC LIBRARIES IN INDIA

1. The enthusiasm of the public in libraries weaned-away after independence. The movement of population from villages to towns and cities; movement of people from place to place for jobs; spread of literacy made existing libraries insufficient to meet their live of literature; lack of proper financial assistance from the governmental agencies forced many of the public libraries to be closed down. One more comment that is often heard is that with the enactment of library legislation, people started feeling that it is now the responsibility of the government to provide library facilities.
2. Though union government has started giving grants to states under different Five Year Plans, the amounts are too meagre to cater the actual needs.
3. RRRLF created by the GOI could not come-up to the expectations as well as needs of the public libraries.
4. The states which enacted library law lost their initial enthusiasm. Out of the 19 states having library legislation seven of the states have not implemented the Act. Some of the acts were about 20 years old. Even in states where there is established structure are starving for literature, staff, accommodation, etc. Due to ban on recruitment, the district and town libraries are being managed by clerks, library/office attendants, etc. Most of the village libraries are managed by a peon or attendant. If he is on leave, the library remains closed.
5. Except some senior citizens, leisured and unemployed no other kind of users makes it a point to visit the libraries.
6. The books are arranged by broad groupings. No classification or cataloguing is done.
7. Not more than 5% of the collection is in use. Majority

of the old books are dumped in dark rooms. No one could dare to enter these rooms. The only items in use are newspapers and magazines. Even newspapers and magazines are very few in the public libraries.

8. Though the GOI wanted that each state should have a State Central Library, about half a dozen states do not have any state central library. Some states declared one of the existing local libraries as State Central Library. Except lending service they are doing nothing worth to be called a SCL.
9. Most of the states have district and/or divisional libraries. Some states have Information Centres of the Government which are also providing the library service.
10. Village or Taluk libraries are under the control of Panchayats or District Education officers. In a couple of states, library service at village level is provided by the school libraries.
11. Some private libraries though economically sound; library service has taken the back-seat. They are interested in increasing their revenue rather than providing quality library services. Some of these libraries are run under the stewardship of a non-matriculate.

CORRECTIVE STEPS NEEDED

Union Government

I. Special initiatives need to be taken for the establishment of State Central Library in each state. Minimum standards need to be established in terms of the collection, services, requirement of space, sections of the library, staff, etc.;

II. A special institute to train library staff need to be established at the national level by the Department of Culture, GOI;

III. A Review Committee needs to be appointed to review the functioning of RRRLF.

IV. Less number of Government officers should be there in the foundation. They seldom attend, yet they influence the functioning a lot;

V. The chairman of the Foundation should be a professional of repute and one with greater enthusiasm and vision.

VI. Foundation should not do the job of book selection. They can at the most circulate lists of books of significance.

VII. State Directorates should prepare plan for the development of libraries in the state. Foundation should consider such proposals objectively.

VIII. Regional offices of the Foundation should be strengthened and the functioning should be decentralized.

State Governments

I. The structure and functioning of libraries need to be reorganized in the light of emerging knowledge society.

II. Apart from books and periodicals, Internet facility, access to databases, multi-media documents, etc. need emphasis in collection development.

III. The environment should be inviting to the users.

IV. There is every need to re-look at the library legislation in the states. Senior professionals should be involved in the revision of the Act. States not having legislation should enact the law.

V. There should a professional Director in each state. All vacancies should be filled-in at the earliest.

SOME GENERAL SUGGESTIONS

I. Each Director of Public Libraries should prepare an annual report, publish and get it approved by the State Library Council. RRRLF should insist on sending a copy of such report to it. A comprehensive report of the Public library situation in the country be prepared by the Foundation and submitted to the Minister of Culture, GOI; Prime Minister; Vice-Chairman, Planning Commission; and to the President of India.

II. "National Commission on Library and Information Services" be appointed at the earliest so that library needs of each section could be taken care of.

16

Library Legislation — Boon or Bane?

DESCENDENC OF THE CONCEPT

Ranganthan's UK Experience

Dr. Ranganathan was in England during 1924 to gain first hand knowledge of organizing libraries. He attended rural library conference in London which gave him an insight into the public library system supported by library legislation. On return to India, he was deeply engaged in organizing Madras University Library. But the idea of library legislation as a means of development of public libraries was simmering in his mind all through.

All Asia Educational Conference, Banaras (1930)

Prof Seshadri was organizing All Asia Education Conference in Banaras in 1930 and requested Ranganathan to organize 'Library Section'. It is at this conference

* Talk delivered at the National Conference on "Reorientation of Library Services in India" organised by A P Library Association between 18-20 August 2007 at Vijayawada.

Ranganathan presented a 'Model Library Act' for discussion. The great library enthusiast Kumara Munindra Deb Rai Mahasai Bengal attended conference. He tried to introduce the library bill of Ranganathan in Bengal Legislature on behalf of Bengal Library Association. But it could not get the approval of the Governor General of India.

Efforts in Madras

The Madras Library Association (MALA) took the business of library legislation seriously. A draft bill was introduced in Madras Legislation in 1933 by *Janab* Basheer Ahmed Sayyed on behalf of MALA. But failed. Second effort was made in 1938, but was withdrawn at the suggestion of Rajaji, the then Premier in the Congress Government in Madras. A third attempt was make once again in Madras in 1946. With the initiative and support of the then Minister in Madras Presidency, Mr. Avinasalingam Chettiar, the bill become the first library act in India in 1948.

Significance of this Act

The first significance is that it was the first Act pertaining to libraries enacted in India. Though the dream of Ranganathan to get the library legislation was enacted by a state in India. It was not in its original form in which he envisaged that it should be. The Madras Library Association was to compromise on many issues in their enthusiasm to get the act passed. The act led to the establishment of a system of libraries in the state with pubic funds. Qualified library staff could be recruited to manage libraries. Quite a good number of new libraries were established, special sections for women, children, physically handicapped could be opened. Mobile library services could be established. Healthy and balanced collections come-up in libraries.

The present position

Today there are 19 states in India, which have enacted library legislation. They are: Madras, Andhra Pradesh,

Chhattisgarh, Karnataka, Maharastra, West Bengal, Manipur, Kerala, Haryana, Mizoram, Goa, Gujarat, Uttaranchal, Rajasthan, and Uttar Pradesh. Records say that Kolhapur state and Hyderabad state also had library acts. These cannot be added to the above because, Kolhapur Act dealt with the Sate Central Library only, but not with the libraries in the entire state. Further, this state and the state of Hyderabad are no more in existence.

Operation of the Acts

Out of the 19 states having library legislation on their statute books, only 8 have a system of public libraries based on library acts. 6 of the states, though enacted library legislation could not commence implementation. Those states that have library legislation in operation could not progress much

How far the Acts succeeded?

1. India's independence and enactment of the first library law coincided. As like in other fields, people started thinking that providing library service is a job of the government. Public participation in establishing and running libraries started declining rapidly.
2. Libraries established under the acts started suffering under bureaucracy.
3. Inaction of the staff under the acts started and public at large decreased significantly.
4. Library staff by and large started feeling that librarianship is merely a source of livelihood rather than service.
5. Collections of cess become a herculean task. Many of the local self- governments are collecting cess, but not returning to local library authorities. This has crippled library services.
6. Constitution of State Library Committees, Local Library Authorities is more on political considerations.

The nominees started playing polities with libraries and library services.

7. Corruption is rampant in recognizing libraries for grants, purchase of books, furniture etc as like in other government departments, sections etc.
8. Lack of sufficient funds made the libraries mere reading rooms of newspapers, magazines, etc. In some libraries books are not added for years.
9. Even in case of states where lump-sum grants are made available, there is no increase in budget allocation for years together.
10. In some states librarian's service is not considered as state service. This resulted in disgruntlement among staff members.
11. No new recruitment against retired staff resulting in service shortage among library personnel. Under employment is also effecting library services.
12. Frequent transfers is not desirable among staff. Personal acquaintance and support between library staff and public at large plays a significant role in library service.
13. Training of library personnel in ICT (Information Communication Technology) is essential.

Some suggestions to ponder with

1. The library legislation on the lines of Model Act of Ranganathan carry no significance. A more objective approach taking into consideration of the new developments in ICT; new forms of documents, new sources of information, various policies of the Union and state governments, new developments at National and international level in library systems and services, new developments in education, mass media etc should be taken in to consideration.

2. Decentralised approach in management of libraries is the need of the hour.
3. There should be more coordination and participation of union and state government, and district or local library unit.
4. Union Government should give grants for purchase of books, equipments etc. The concerned state government should provide funds mainly to meet the salaries of the staff. Local bodies should meet the running cost of building (including repair), electricity, etc.
5. A state level training school for providing in service training to staff needs to be established.
6. Union Government should draw plans for networking of public libraries in the country.
7. Union catalogues of various information sources be compiled, maintained and updated at the state level.
8. A National Commission on Libraries and Information Services be established at the union level to monitor and advice the government.
9. The role played by RRRLF be reviewed and it be reoriented to the changed circumferences.

17

Community Information and Changing Role of Libraries*

LIBRARY AS A COMMUNITY CENTRE IN THE PAST

The Public Library has been playing an important role as a community centre right from the beginning. It has taken-up the role of providing information to all classes, all castes and all categories of villagers- the literate, illiterate as well as neo- literate. It has been providing books and other reading material to the literates, reading out newspapers, conducting adult education classes, etc. for illiterates and special material to neo- literates.

Every possible opportunity was ceased to publicise the library and its services and satisfied the information needs of the entire community.

---

* Talk delivered at the National Seminar on "Community Information Services" held at Tenali between 9-10 March, 2002.

Public Library Today

The public library of today is meeting the information needs of the society by providing books, periodicals etc. for adults - men and women, children; community information to all sections of the society; special needs of students, unemployed, minorities, etc. Branch libraries and mobile libraries took libraries closer to the society. With the advent of audio and video documents, libraries started stocking these in a good number.

PUBLIC LIBRARY *VS* MASS MEDIA

Mass media like, newspapers and magazines; radio and television have been posing a threat to the very existence of the public library. However, public library stood the onslaught of other print and non- print media which have an access to the drawing rooms of the public. Public libraries changed a lot to meet the changing needs of its users.

It has started giving room to the print as well as not-print media under its roof. Still a large number of population deprieved of the new sources of information can have access only through the library. The new print and non- print media cannot provide 'personalised' service which only a library could do.

CHANGING ROLE OF LIBRARIES

Further, some of the public libraries changed their concept from providing only documentary sources of information to meeting every community need- say providing tools and kits for domestic use; wall- hangings; baby- sitting, etc.

NEW CHALLENGES AND NEED FOR CHANGE IN ROLES

The present age is called 'information age'. It is now axiomatic that our economy is shifting from one driven by industry to one driven by information. For two hundred years we have used paper and paper based documents for recording and communicating information. In the 'information society' most of information will be communicated through computers, networks - wired or unwired. The information will be cheaper, occupies less space and communicated with great speed.

Information as a Commodity

Some view information as a 'commodity' and use this perception to make a case for regulating its flow just as other commodities are regulated. Apart from providing public services, it has become imperative for the governments to provide precise, concise and upto date information as an input for production, distribution, well- being of the society as well as social upliftment.

THE NEW ROLE OF THE LIBRARY

The Role of the library in the 'information society' is varied, more challenging and diverse.

Position of the Library

In the new emerging information system, the administrators have to decide whether the library is to be a part of the information system in a village or the library should be the hub of the entire information system of the village. The LIS profession should try to work for radiating all information services at the local level through the library. The society and the information needs of the users are fast changing and it is time for the libraries to act quickly and prove the role the libraries can play in the 'information society'j

The Kerala Example

Use of Information Technology (IT) for rural development was initiated in 1997. In Ernakulam District which has the distinction of being the first district in the country to achieve 100% literacy was chosen for the IT experiment. Under this project, all the departments at the Panchayat level in 20 selected Panchayats were collected through volunteers and entered the data in Malayalam using a phonetic key-board. An information network was created at each Panchayat. Now this information base is being used for decentrialised planning in vogue in Kerala. This scheme is named as the Information Kerala Mission (KM) and is slated to cover all the 990 Panchayats in the State.

Under this programme a computer with Internet facility is located in the Local Library and is jointly managed by the Panchayat and the Dept. of Information Technology, Govt. of kerala. The centre is named as "Sevana" which provides the following information:

1. Welfare programmes of the government;
2. Application forms for various support programmes;
3. Information about universities, colleges, schools etc.-qualification required, admission procedures, etc., including results;
4. Tourism;
5. Electronic telephone directory;
6. Public Service Commission information, Employment information;
7. Question banks for competitive examinations;
8. Career guidance;
9. Air and rail timings etc.

These centres are expected to organise 'awareness' programmes for public.

The library is thus chosen as a nodal point for providing community information in Kerala.

Information Technology (IT) in Other States

Andhra Pradesh : The thrust in IT applications in AP

is on e- governance. Computer network is used for recording data of commercial taxes, excise, treasuries, transport, etc, and their application. Hyderabad is connected with all district headquarters enabling video- conferencing facility. Land records have been computerised to a large extend. It has a plan to link all 1125 Mandals in the State. It is proposed to computerise 7.67 crore citizen records, 1.2 crore land records and 1.67 crore household records.

The Duggirala Citizens Information System in AP proved that telecentres can be effectively operated by NGOs.

Karnataka : Karnataka provided leadership in IT in India. There are about 822 software companies exporting IT goods worth 1.2 billion during 1999-2000. It has initiated Gram panchayat Information System (GPIS) in 1999 with a pilot project at Bellandur near Bangalore. It is expected that GPIS will have records of roads, water supply, irrigation, rainfall, etc, vital for planning. This information is to be made accessible to public through the "Gram Panchayat Information Kiosks".

Madhya Pradesh : Though, nearly half of the population is below povertyline in MP, it has taken lead role in taking IT to various parts of the State under its "Gyandoot" (= Internet) programme. A pilot project was initiated in the Dhar district of MP wherein 311 Gram Panchayats extending over 600 villages covering about 5 lakh population. This Intranet link is connected to the Internet. The corresponding Internet web-site is GYANDOOT. NET. This network is providing prices and volumes of local markets, land records, public information, etc. E-mail replies are provided for public queries.

Other States : Almost all states have taken IT initiatives in a big or small way. Thus, the changes are going to be fast and conspicuous. A couple of projects worth mentioning here are "Information Village Project" in Pondichery initiated by

M S Swaminathan Research Foundation and IDRC, Canada; and Warna Wired Village Project implemented by NIC, Pune; Govt. of Maharashtra; and Warna Cooperative Society.

CONCLUSION

1. It is going to have a great sway in governance, trade, commerce, education, entertainment and enlightenment of the citizen. It is heartening to note the approach of the Kerala Government, wherein the village library has been taken as the hub of IT activities and dissemination of information to the public. The other states should also try to adopt the model of Kerala government.
2. Government should not take-up the direct responsibility of providing information of general interest to its agencies. It should carry on its official work alone through its nodal agencies at the village level.
3. Voluntary agencies (= NGOs) should also initiate steps in gethering, processing and disseminating local information. They should do this through the local library.
4. Govt. of India should evolve a system of providing access to information at local level through libraries taking note of experiments carried out by different state governments and NGOs.
5. The traditional library services are to be integrated with digital information services.

SOURCE MATERIAL

1. Than, A and Vijayadharan, D., IT Landscape in India etc. Hyderabad: CRUST, 2001.
2. Comhsol Software (Pvt Ltd.). Electronic governance solutions from COMPHSOL. http:// www.compusol@fcvsnl.com

3. Parthasarth, A., E- governing in god's own country. *The Hindu*, 16th Nov. 2000.
4. Andhra Pradesh, First IT Policy 2000. Hyderabad, 2000.
5. Madhya Pradesh, Gyandoot. http://gyandoot.net/gyandoot/Internet.html.

School

18

Ranganathan and School Library*

ROLE OF A SCHOOL LIBRARY

1. Stimulating the self-educability of each student; and
2. Helping each student to develop along his own lines, at his own speed to his own fullness.

EARLY EXPERIENCE OF RANGANATHAN

Ranganathan joined Government College, Coimbatore as a Lecturer in July, 1920. He found the college library not suited for student centred or library centred teaching. He prepared a long list of essential books and requests the Principal for purchase of the books. Reluctantly, the Principal purchased the books. Those books were kept in the class room. Students were given assignments and were asked to answer by using the books. At the end of the year the results proved that the approach of Ranganathan was correct. 17

---

* Text of Lecture delivered at the "Orientation for Central School Librarians" organised in Nagpur in May-June 2003.

out of the 19 students passed. 10 of them with distinction in his subject. Even the university first was from his college.

EFFORTS OF RANGANATHAN IN MADRAS

Lectures on 'School Lib' at Teachers Training College

Discussion for one hour on each Friday during Second Term.

'Library Hours' were made compulsory in 1933 in Madras Presidency Training College for Teachers.

Not many qualified librarians as on today. One of the teacher was asked to look after the Library and conduct Library Hours.

1934 Ranganathan was asked to conduct a training programme for school teachers. MALA and University of Madras conducted courses from 1935-1937.

Report to cover Library Work in Schools

Inspection Reports were made to cover a short account on Library Work in schools.

Origin of School Libraries

Wood's Despatch suggested for libraries in schools.

Books to suppliment text books started appearing.

Co-ordination of Class Room Work with School Library Work.

What is Education?

Plato — 'Fitting the individual to community life.'

Thomas Moore — 'Giving a grind in classes.'

John Dewery — 'Transmission of the acquired powers to the new generation in order to secure the continued existence and growth of community.'

Ranganathan — 'Releasing and exercising the creative ability of each.'

Need for School Libraries/Library Hours in Schools

1. Rate of change in the volume of facts, information and ideas;
2. Limit to the holding capacity of the brain; and
3. Over loaded curriculum, a chronic feature.

Overloading of curriculum cause damage to self-confidence and natural capacity of the student.

Postulate 1 : "Each student should be inducted in the use of current facts, ideas and information tailored to his needs and capacity."

Postulate 2 : "Replace 'no change' by 'change'.

Postulate 3 : "Divide facts, ideas and information into two varieties :

1. Those to be carried in memory; and
2. Those to be found out when necessary from Reference books.

Postulate 4 : "School education should train the students in 'Reference method'."

Postulate 5 : 'The term 'Book' transcends the term 'Textbook'.

'Teaching is not dictation of notes'

"Socialisation of Books"

Reference works provide "Externalised Memory".

Books need to be socialised. Socialisation of books leads to "Socialisation of Knowledge".

NEW EDUCATION

Camel Theory of Education ousted out.

New Education would change the whole outlook on education and its methods in particular.

1. Students would not be kept passively receptive.

2. No student would be able to thinking of something else, though appeearently listening to the teacher's words.
3. Each student would be made the chief actor in the arena.
4. The curiosity of each student would be kindled instead of being smoothered by his being thrown into a passive mood devoid of much interest in the words reaching his ears.
5. Enquiring and exploring attitude in each student would be roused in the measure of his interest.
6. Teaching the 'Method of finding out' would be half the task of education.
7. To teach a method would be providing opportunities for applying it.
8. Provide opportunity to students to find out' facts, ideas and information.
9. After arousing curiosity the student should be thrown amidist the books in the Library.
10. The Librarian and the teacher should plan helping the student enjoy his work in the Library.
11. The help should be in the form of:
    (i) Guiding the student to reach his / her book(s)
    (ii) Training in taking the relevant notes
    (iii) Teach them to weave these notes into a whole.

Examination is not testing the Memory but to test one's ability to conduct himself successfully in situations in life.

"Library will be a Workshop in a school adopting New Education."

John Dewery & New Education

Experiments at University Elementary School at Chicago with 15 children in January 1896. He introduced

Supervised Study; Project Method; Contract Technique, etc.

He thus, introduced the Library Centred Education.

In New Education there may or may not be a library hour, the Library is an open house for the students.

The students should have freedom in the Library. Open any almyrah, pull-out any book, and access for selection.

A student trained in the pedestrian stream of education could not develop individuality and independent thinking and be creative.

Richard Haldane said - School was indeed never an interesting period to me."

Driving out the fear of the school

1. How to avoid students not coming to school?
2. How to make teaching interesting ?
3. How to avoid suppression of creativeness in students;
4. How to avoid development of anti-social tendencies in students.

LIBRARY

Place for writing books Place for storing books. A collection of books. Accessible collection of books. Books for All.

Constituents

Books

Users (Readers)

Staff

Books

Text books and Normal books on all subjects

Informative (biographies, travels, etc)

Supplementary (Digests, commentaries, etc)

Recreative

Reference

Inspirational (Religion, philosophy, etc)

Adventure

Students for a Good Book

Contents & narration (Intellectual Standard)

Language & style (Linguistic Standard)

(Qualitative Standard -) Paper, printing, illustrations, typography etc.

Fugitive Material

Pamphlets, folders, plans, pictures, posters, prints, clippings

Extention Work

Other than printed works (non-book material) Service to teachers (Supplementary & extra - reading) Extending service to public.

Human Constituents

Students

Attracting students by providing :

1. Books of interest
2. Books of recency
3. Books of novelty

Making willing beneficiaries

Sympathetic service

Exact service

Prompt service

Continuous service

Teachers

Should help the Library Staff in :

1. Book selection
2. Publicity
3. Class Room Work

Library Staff

Qualifications

Status

Material Constituent

Building - Stack, Reading hall, Seminar - Group study, Counter, Staff

Open access

Gangways

Floor Level

Ventilation & Light

Aesthetics

Functioning

Creating Library habit

Care of books

Library organisation

Library Rules

Use

Discipline

Use of books, holding, reading, no markings

Messages

through leaflets

talks

pictorial appeals

Help in preparation

(1) *Pre-class Library Work* (calling out information on the topics)

Help from teacher & library staff

Group / Team Work

Sub areas divided among the students & hunt for information.

(2) *Parallel Reading*

Library (record the search procedure, material gathered, etc) Librarian should gather such books and keep at a corner for the benefit of students.

(3) *Follow-up Work*

Supplementary reading Special care of average student

Extra-Moral Stimulus

Celebration of recurring and isolated events & festivals of local, national and international events.

(1) Special topical sequence
(2) Special lists of books for distribution
(3) Arrange special talks
(4) Special exhibition if needed
(5) Involve students to organise the event / speak on the occasion.
(6) Special Story Hours
   (i) Folk method (*Katha, Kalakshepa, Puran, Pravachan* etc)
   (ii) Story with music
   (iii) Book display linked with story telling

Training in Fact Finding

Special collection of books of informative nature

('How to do it' series; 'Travel & tours'; 'Nature'; 'Fairs & Festivals'; etc)

- inspirative books

(Religion, Philosophy, biology, history & adventure etc)

Inculcating Library Habit

Learning by experience

Formal Lessons

Supervised Study (assignments to be worked out under the supervision of the librarian)

Project Method (individual or group)

Maintenance of Diaries

(i) Fact finding

(ii) Diary of recreative books (date of commencement, completion, no of hours, etc)

(iii) Diary for inspirational passages

Social Role of School Library

Civics in action

Public mindedness - careful handling of books, cleanliness, silence

Consideration for others - misplacement, period of loan, mutilation

Respect for rule

Right habits

Fire prevention

Personal manners - noise, placing books, disguesting actions in reading

Room

Reference Service

Initiation of students - Book and its pens, Library routines, Lib tools, Notes taking bibliography, talks, apprenticeship, observation, Service to individual students, Service to the class.

Course

Care / Rules / Make-up of Book / Ref books / Periodicals etc

Ref Service - Long, Ready etc. Hub of Lib Work

Lib Rules with stress on penal classes

Catalogue / classification / shelf arrangement / circulation

College

19

Electronic Media and College Library*

ROLE OF ELECTRONIC MEDIA

Electronic media has changed the scene of not only libraries, but also educational system as a whole. In a college it is extensively used in libraries; general administration;.and teaching in class room. It all started with mechanization, then automation, computerization, multimedia, use of Internet, networking, office automation, use of Educational Technology in the class room. Let us see these developments in brief and their role in a college library, more so in a rural college library.

COMPUTERIZATION

It is now common to find fully or partially computerised systems for acquisition, cataloguing, indexing,

---

* Keynote Address delivered at the State Level Conference on "Impact on Electronic Media on Rural College Libraries" held at Govindra Warjuirkar Arts and Commerce College and Postgraduate Study Centre, Nagbhid (MS) on 29 Jan 2010.

file construction, information retrieval, documentary products (bulletins, indexes, SDI, etc.), loan operations, data retrieval and exploitation, and routine control and administrative operations.

Computer systems, however, have to be designed, maintained, fed with information and used by people. In other words, they do not simply replace human beings but instead call for a high level of qualification and at least as much, though admittedly different, work for advantage to be taken of their enormous processing capacity.

Impact

A process of great change is taking place in library and information systems as a result of computer application and information systems as a result of computer and information technology. Modern technology is ending to alter radically the nature of our society and affect the prevailing economic, political, and social values. Library and information systems are also, in the process, required to change, improve and adapt to new conditions. A new wave of information technology, based on electronics, is forcing library and information systems to undergo a major transformation. In Western industrialised countries, libraries and information centres have been quick to realise that, in the context of stock of knowledge enlarging so rapidly in a post-industrialised society, classical approaches relating to storage, retrieval and utilization of information were no longer adequate and that an effective solution lay in making fullest use of new developments in electronics, computer, telecommunication, micro-recording, etc.

INFORMATION TECHNOLOGY

Concept

Information Technology (IT) is electronic technologies used for collecting, storing, processing and communicating information. There are two main categories - those which process information (such as computer systems); and those which disseminate information (such as telecommunication systems). It has a wider connotation for libraries which include in addition technologies like, repro-micrographic technology, technical communication technologies; and database creation and use.

The term 'Information Technology' is widely used in UK, USA and India; 'Telematics' is used for same in France and 'Informatics' is widely used in Russia and other socialist countries.

Scope

Dr. S.S. Murthy says that Information Technology is operative in the following environments :

1. **Library Management** : Classification, cataloguing, indexing, database creation, CAS,SDI, etc;
2. **Library Automation** : Organising databases and automating library housekeeping operations;
3. **Library Networking** : Resource sharing and information dissemination;
4. **Reprography** : Photography, microfilms, microfiche, audio and video tapes, printing, optical, etc; and
5. **Technical Communication** : Technical writing, editing, publishing, DTP systems, etc.

Jennifer Rowley outlined the following four areas of Information Technology:

1. **Methods and tools for recording of knowledge** : Computer storage media (such as magnetic tapes, discs, etc); optical storage media (such as CDs); and products like full-text databases etc;
2. **Methods of keeping records** : Computer hardware, software, designing, creating and editing databases, etc;

3. **Methods of indexing documents and information:** Computerised indexes and index files; large machine readable catalogues, network of libraries; and
4. **Methods of communicating knowledge :** Electronic mail, facsimile transmission, electronic journals, teleconferencing, and data communication networks,

Impact

The information Technology has a wide ranging impact on library and information work.

The Electronic Library

The Electronic Library is a storehouse of information, documents, audio-visual and graphic materials stored in a variety of media ranging from printed books, periodicals, posters and reports, microforms, slides, films, videos, audio discs, audio tapes, optical discs, magnetic tapes, floppy discs, etc. Electronic Library of the future is likely to be part of a network. In theory, it is only necessary for one electronic copy of a document to be stored in the whole world. A world electronic library would be a possibility.

An electronic library deals with both housekeeping operations like acquisitions, catalogue creation, circulation control, serial control. Online Public Access Catalogues (OPAC) and the generation of management information; and information retrieval systems like external databases and associated services and products and internal or local databases and their associated services and products. The associated services include Current Awareness Services (CAS), Selective Dissemination of Information(SDI), etc.

Online searching of external databases has been available since the early 1960s.

Impact of New Technologies on Libraries

Information activities have undergone rapid transformations from conventional methods, consequent upon introduction of new technologies. This is summarised as follows:

Information Activity	Conventional Method	New Technology
Generate, Originate	Writing, Typing	Word processing, Text editing, Character Recognition, Voice Recognition.
Preserve, Store	Manuscript Paper-print media	Electronic publishing, Magnetic storage, Videotext, Tele-text, Computer disk, ROM
Process	Classification, Cataloguing,	Electronic data Processing, Artificial Intelligence/Expert Systems.
Retrieval	Catalogues, Indexes	Database Management Systems, Information Retrieval-off-line, on line.
Disseminate	Lists, Bibliographies Communicate Abstracts, Hard copies	Electronic mail, Electronic document Delivery, Computer Conferencing, Telefacsmile, view data.
Destroy	Physical Weeding	Magnetic erasers Optical erasers, Re-use the medium.

Areas of Computer Application

The areas of computer application in library and information field may be enumerated as follows:

I. Database Activity

- Creation of local databases
- online access to remote databases
- use of external databases on local computer
- downloading of information for referral service
- current awareness service/SDI reference service

- compilation of bibliographies
- bibliometric studies

II. Library

- cataloguing and catalogue production
- indexing and production of indexes
- union catalogues
- bibliographies
- directories and inventories
- thesaurus construction
- serials control
- Circulation
- acquisition

III. Management Information System/Decision Support System

- computing
- statistical manipulation
- tabulations
- graphics
- simulation
- expert system and artificial intelligence
- bureautics

IV. Data Communication and Networking

- electronic mail
- messaging system teleconferencing
- video/teletext

V. Other Applications

- electronic publishing
- document delivery
- translation

INTERNET

Internet, particularly the web is a wonderful source of information that can vastly improve the array of resources available to users. Both libraries, students as well as teachers can make best use of this unlimited source of information. Internet connects various networks around the globe operated by different organisations. Internet started in late 1960s at U.S. Defence Department Agency. The network developed by Bot Baranek and Newman in 1969 heralded yet another revolution in information communication. This has led to a new technology called World Wide Web in 1993.

WORLD WIDE WEB

Web is a series of interconnected documents stored on computer sites to web sites. On the Internet via web more and more linked data are available at a very high speed. When the operator uses a computer, it sends a software programme called 'browser' to search on the 'home page' of another computer. The home-page gives the organization or individual name of (the sponsor website) and displays a list of highlighted words, or buttons by clicking a mouse pointer.

INTRANET

Intranet is developed by using network technology to deliver information over the network only accessible to employees or the invited users. Intranets are used for transferring information within an organisation. The information in an intranet is secured and contained within the organisation.

e-mail

E-mail transmits the written message via computers connected on network. E-mail through Intranet transmits messages from and to various sectors like government agencies, educational institutions, business houses as well as individuals. Internet providers generally allow one to created an e-mail ID (or address) and send or receive messages.

MULTIMEDIA

Multimedia is a combination of some or all forms such as text, data images, photographs, animation, audio and video, which are converted from different formats into a uniformat digital media and is delivered by computers. Unlike the analogue media, the digital media which allows users to manipulate according to the needs. Use at their pace, and interact at any point of the program when a multimedia program is developed in a hypertext environment, the resulting product is called 'hypermedia'. So multimedia would then be a part of the hypermedia products but not vice-versa. The basic difference between these two is in the organisation and linkage of the information fragments. The information fragments in multimedia are organized linearly whereas in hypermedia, these are non-linealy organized with links to each other.

The main elements of the multimedia are:

(i) **Text :** Information about an object or event etc. Notes, captions, subtitles, contents, indexes, dictionaries and help facilities.

(ii) **Data :** Tables, charts, graphs, spreadsheets, statistics and raw data.

(iii) **Graphics :** Both traditional and computer generated such as drawings, points, maps, etc.

(iv) **Photographic images :** Negatives, slides, prints, video cameras, etc.

(v) **Animation :** Including both computer generated, video etc.

(vi) **Audio :** It includes speech and music digitised form cassettes, tapes, CDs etc.

(vii) **Video :** Either converted from analogue film of entirely created within a computer.

Impact of Multimedia on Library Services

Multimedia, not only helps the users in providing information from different media on one platform, but also saves on space, money, maintenance, operational inconveniences etc. The major advantages of multimedia in libraries are:

(a) It can help satisfying different information needs such as reference, enrichment, entertainment, leisure, etc.

(b) It can help meeting various types of information preference of the users such as scholarly, scientific, vocational, artistic, recreational, etc.

(c) Being a digital format, information can also be accessed by remote users on a network. It also helps in overcoming to accommodate users.

(d) It is interesting and easy to use over the existing form such as print microforms, online etc.

(e) Its control and interactivity helps the users and provides the benefits of books and human beings.

ELECTRONIC DOCUMENTS

E-Books

Electronic publishing has led to new opportunities to deliver information. In many cases, it has created opportunities for writers, who otherwise might not get their work exposed to a wide audience, or who might not gain the chance to publish through the traditional channels provided by mainstream print publishing. Journals have been published electronically since the beginning of the 1990s, yet only recently have publishers begun to make books available electronically. A number of electronic publishers have emerged; plus well known publishers of print materials, including Oxford University Press and Princenton

University Press, have started to experiment with electronic publishing. Electronic publishing creates opportunities for users as well as authors and publishers. Many of the electronic books or electronic publishers' Web sites freely permit and encourage readers to provide feedback on works, often directly to the author rather than to the publisher. This chapter will explore electronic publishing projects and electronic journals.

Mc Carry (1997) outlines examples of electronics books and monographs :

- Edited books appearing online for the first time, such as Pery Willett's Victorian Woman Writers Project;
- Re-edited books based on print editions such as Ian Lancashire's Project Representative Poetry, a collection of about 730 poems by about 80 poets, ranging from Wyatt to Swinburne;
- Post print by authors which are online re-issues of books previously published in print and for which the author still holds the copyright (examples include Cassidorous by James J O'Donnell);
- Post print by editors which include items faithfully reproduced as possible without significant re-editing of the text (example include Coulmbia University's Project Bartelby.)
- Electronic books also includes versions which are available simultaneously in print and on the web, at books distributed on CD-ROMS or floppy disks.

E-Journals

There is an exponential growth in the number of electronic journals, newsletters and academic discussion lists. The ARL Directory (1997) contains 1465 titles as electronic journals. There are 1049 peer-reviewed journals compared to 417 in the 1996 edition. The number of electronic journals increased to 700 titles in the 5th edition in 1995, from 440 in the 4th edition in 1994 and 110 in the first edition in 1991 respectively. Since electronic journals are proliferating extensively, they appear in most academic disciplines. The major broad categories are: Science, Technology and Social Sciences. World Wide Web (WWW) and the Internet technology offer the possibility of using computers and communication networks to create alternative electronic forms for wider distribution and access.

Electronic Journals - Benefits and limitations

The advantages of electronic journals can be summarized as:

(a) Electronic journals allow for more speed in the scientific communication process.

(b) It is possible to add experimental data, software and even multimedia extensions.

(c) Electronic journals demand neither library space nor shelving costs nor can they be stolen from the library.

(d) Electronic journals are available 24 hours a day, 7 days a week.

(e) Articles can be linked with the body of scholarly literature.

(f) There is a provision for a more open peer review process.

(g) The cost of the electronic journals is likely to be less than its print version in future depending on the availability of both the versions.

CONSORTIA APPROACH

Consortia are nothing but cooperative effort, which manages ail the library services collectively. It has the purpose of exploring the need for libraries to make the most effectiveness of their funds collectively. This partnership fosters pride, determination and a sense of ownership between its constituent libraries and staff. Consortia are regarded as an effective strategy to increase the buying power of individual libraries over the short term and an opportunity to maximize the efforts of cooperative collection building for resource sharing over the long term (Richer, 1999). It is essential to understand the definition of the term consortium which is a powerful cooperative strategy.

The following definitions from the available sources are the derivation from the basic term of "consortium".

A Consortium is said to be "a cooperative arrangement among groups or institutions, or an association or society" (American Heritage Dictionary).

Consortia in India

Libraries are taking the consortia to which they belong a great deal more seriously, then was the case a few years back. This offer libraries the ability to give users the access they are coming to expect and demand to a much broader range of materials than any one library could possibly offer.

Specific Consortia

1. FORSA (Forum for Resource Sharing in Astronomy)
2. INDEST(Indian Digital Library in Engineering Science and Technology)
3. IIM Libraries Consortia
4. INFONET of UGC and INFLIBNET
5. CSIR Consortium
6. ICICI Knowledge Park
7. SNDT/LISA Consortium

ELECTRONIC OFFICE

Offices are also concerned with information storage and retrieval. Hence, IT is widely used in offices. An office is a place where people read, think, write and communicate. A number of devices were introduced in offices. For example, the word processor was seen as a substitute for the typewriter and computers are used for filing of records. The new technology affected the organization and nature of work in offices. New technology has freed office work from its focus on the flow of paper between people and allowed the focus of activities to shift to the transaction recorded in the computers and the people making decisions and performing various tasks. It enabled faster decision-making, elimination of redundant work and better utilization of human resources.

Computerized Information Systems

Various computerized systems of use in management are:

1. Transaction Processing Systems (TPS);
2. Management Information System(MIS);
3. Decision Support System(DSS);
4. Office Automation System (OAS); and
5. Executive Support System (ESS)

MEDIA SERVICES

In order to coalesce library and teaching in the college, following media services could be introduced by the library.

Closed Circuit Televisions (CCTV)

In order to facilitate services to media class room needs, a CCTV system should be installed and class rooms should be equipped with monitors and control panels. Faculty members should be encouraged to use this system which they are planning to show a film, or video-tape. With this system, there is no need to set-up and operate a projector, no unwanted noise from the projector, and light can be kept on the note-taking. If it is a monitor equipped classroom, the teacher can directly contact CC room simply by picking up the telephone receiver of the control panel in the class-room.

Telecourse Viewing

Telecourse tapes can be made available for review by

students on video-tape machines. Now-a-days, CD is one of the best media for recording and dissemination.

GRAPHIC AREA

In the graphic area a wide range of material like slides, original photographs, over head transparencies, original art works, filmstrip, duplication, charts, posters, graphs, layouts for publications etc., can be provided.

Production Guide

This area provides many production related media services. These include off-air taping of cable programming, video-production of lectures, meetings, speeches, and special presentations, audio production, video duplication and audio duplication.

CONCLUSION

Thus library can not only provide traditional library services, but also help making teaching more effective, learner oriented, bring live displays to the class-room and make learning quick and enjoyable.

Thus library can and should become the hub of teaching-learning process of college irrespective, of its location urban or rural.

20

Re-engineering of College Library Services

DIGITAL AGE

The advent of microcomputer, optical disk and other mass storage media, world wide packet networks and communication technology, digital image technology, graphic and compression technologies have dramatically changed the way we live, we think, we communicate and we use and view technologies.

The present 'information age' with electronic and digital environment resulting in 'information super-highway' made virtually the world a 'global village'. The day is not far where there will be 'one world-one library' where information is accessible wherever it is, by any one and at any time.

---

* Keynote Address delivered at the National Seminar on "Reengineering of College Library Services" held at New Arts, Commerce and Science College, Wordha on 6 Feb. 2011.

VARIED SOURCES OF INFORMATION

Abundant information available on net and the World Wide Web (WWW) is enabling seekers of information to gather, collect and consume. Apart from net; huge volume of information is available in CDs, DVDs, Network Accessed Storages (NASs), databases, digitized documents in addition to print forms. Thus, librarians have to possess adequate knowledge of handling traditional print and non-print and meta-documents. Librarians should be ahead of their users.

In electronic forms, the users also need to be adept in access, processing and retrieve information. Most of them do possess needed information handling techniques. If librarians want to be leaders in the age of ICT, must master the skills and they should be ahead of their clientele.

IMPACT OF NEW TECHNOLOGY ON LIBRARIES

Changes in information technology have generated corresponding changes in society, higher education and libraries as following :

- Shift from paper based resources to electronic one,
- Shift from acquisition to accessing the resources,
- Media convergence in digital resources,
- Knowledge about web page designing and e-journals is essential,
- User demands for access facilities in his place, at his desktop,
- Growing importance of consortia agreements for journal subscription,
- Provision of resource sharing to overcome budgetary constraint;
- Maintaining LAN, WAN, Internet and intranet facilities with faster access;

- Getting access to e-books, e-journals and e-library projects,
- Increase of E-mail, domain based Internet browsing and access to on-line resources apart from OPAC in the libraries.

USER EXPECTATIONS FROM THE LIBRARY

These are verbatum responses by patrons who were asked what they expected from their libraries:

- Everything in full-text and downloadable or printable;
- Faster service;
- 24/7 service availability;
- Easy access;
- Virtual reference service librarian available online 24/7;
- Easy-to-use Web resources permitting self service;
- A Librarian who knows all subjects and all databases;
- Everything should be in electronic format;
- Several options/ alternatives to choose from;
- A Web site that works;
- Ability to conduct all library transactions online (like : library registration, request documents delivery and inter library loan, renew library items, etc.); and
- A Web site search engine that can find what a user want.

CHANGING ROLE OF LIBRARIES

The new technology as we have been made greater impact on the structure, functioning and services of libraries. Library service is no more confined to the four walls of the library. Paper - based documents are supplanted by electronic and digital resources. In the new environment user-librarian interaction is reduced to the minimum.

Users are adapted to the use of electronic sources of information. Library may at most become an intermediary in the information transfer chain. In future users can have direct access to the source and the library may conveniently be bypassed. It is in this context librarians have to re-orient their services to provide easy access and conserve the time of research potential. Users need not commute to the library for information. Library of the future will be a reprocessing center where information is gathered, processed, packaged in a suitable way so that the packet contains information tailor made to the needs of the users.

The electronic libraries will need to provide a range of new value added services for internally generated and externally acquired information. The cost of operations in future electronic libraries will be high and the investment will be continuous. Thus, the cost of information will be high as against the one time investment on documents in a traditional library.

SKILL REQUIREMENT FOR THE LIBRARY PROFESSIONALS

The collision of the increasing diversity of users needs and the digital environment made the librarians to acquire new competencies and skills regarding-

- New technological innovations such as INTERNET 2, Professional skills with practical approach,
- Cataloguing of web resources using metadata standards,
- Web page designing and maintenance,
- Preservation of digital resources,
- Data base creation and various models of it,
- Attending to the trouble shooting systems,
- Scanning, indexing, conversion and linkage issues,

- To work in the digital environment by using it today,
- Turning to the new environment by using IT tools,
- User awareness to the library resources and services,
- Accessibility of information on-line,
- Improving the communication skill among the staff, with user and the top management,
- Strengthening of librarians skills in dealing with copyright and negotiating with publishers,
- High priority must be given to staff development,
- Through task skill training, boot camps, workshop on different themes; and
- Demonstration of IT. products, seminars and webinars on staff competency.

FUTURE OF THE LIBRARY

The future library will have to provide information not only of academic/research nature but also processed information for planning, organization, administration of the parent organization itself. In a college library it should function as a resource centre for teaching-learning and research needs.

The serendipity or the chance discovery of information useful to a researcher has become the important task. In the print-only days researchers would browse journals near by on the shelves, however the electronic environment does not lend itself well to that type of browsing. This role continues to be a niche for librarians, to develop innovative methods to facilitate the information harvesting such as metadata, net scrape, www.mosoic, the URL structures, the dot com etc.

In the place of traditional functions, processes and procedures such as cataloging, circulation OPAC, creating conventional database etc. the libraries need to use the new exciting technologies in the areas of access and retrieval, creating institutional repositories, archiving and preservation of rare and valuable documents by way of digitization, user driven services and publications, etc.

In order to supply access to information rather than acquiring, libraries can use consortia-power to obtain better prices for information. By developing diversified programs we can attract partnership between entrepreneurs, government schools, the media etc. They have to now apply the principles of e-commerce as cost- effectiveness and efficiencies become increasingly important for the survival and thriving libraries. The future library is going to be a 24×7 accessible entity unlike 10 am to 5 pm earlier. A large number of users can access information from anywhere, at any time. The library systems will become more user-friendly.

EMERGING CONCEPTS

21

Information Literacy : Concept and Scope

LITERACY

The term 'Literacy' came from 'Letters'. Literate is one who will be able to read and write. There are some more related terms like literature (written works especially fiction, poetry, drama, etc.) Literati (educated people). The extension of the terms literacy include the ability to understand and interpret specific concept or phenomenon. To be literate one should have the capacity to write and communicate; read, interpret and assimilate information; or communicate the same to others.

INFORMATION

In simple terms 'information' is the processed data. Data may be a statement, fact, concept or an association of

* Keynote Address delivered at the Workshop on "Information Literacy" organised by Department of Library and Information Science, RTM Nagpur University in association with SALIS on 28 December 2006.

statements, opinions or ideas. Information in one sense is a raw material which has the potential of interpretation which when received by a person becomes knowledge. Information has the potential to solve problems and add value in decision making.

KNOWLEDGE AND INFORMATION

Knowledge and information are often used interchangeably. Farradane makes difference between these two terms. According to him information is physical surrogate of knowledge (i.e. language) used for communication. While knowledge is memorable records of a process in the brain, something available in the mind; production of consciousness in the mind is at present quite unexplained.

McGarry summarizes varied attributes to see the nature of information.

(1) Information can be regarded as a near synonym of fact.

(2) It has a transforming or reinforcing effect on what is known, or believed to be known, by a human being.

(3) Information is used as an aid to decision-making.

(4) Information is the freedom of choice one has in selecting a message.

(5) Information is a necessary piece of something when we are faced with a choice, the amount required depends upon the complexity of decision to be made.

UNIVERSE OF KNOWLEDGE

Universe of knowledge is the sum total of the knowledge conserved by human beings. The knowledge in the human brain dies with the individual. It is in this context recording and communication to posterify in the written form has gained importance. In the beginning knowledge was communicated from the preceptor to pupil by *sruti-smriti* (repetition and recording in memory).

RECORDING OF KNOWLEDGE

In order to give permanence to human thought lettering' was developed. Initially the recording was done on stone, hence they were called *Akshara* (that cannot be wiped off).

LIBRARY AS A COMMUNITY CENTRE IN THE PAST

The Public Library has been playing an important role as a community centre right from the beginning. It has taken-up the role of providing information to all classes, all castes and all categories of villagers- the literate, illiterate as well as neo- literate. It has been providing books and other reading material to the literates, reading out newspapers, conducting adult education classes, etc. for illiterates and special material to neo- literates.

Every possible opportunity was ceased to publicise the library and its services and satisfied the information needs of the entire community.

PUBLIC LIBRARY TODAY

The public library of today is meeting the information needs of the society by providing books, periodicals etc. for adults - men and women, children, community information to all sections of the society; special needs of students, unemployed, minorities, etc. Branch libraries and mobile libraries took libraries closer to the society. With the advent of audio and video documents, libraries started stocking these in a good number.

NEW CHALLENGES AND NEED FOR CHANGE IN ROLES

The present age is called 'information age'. It is now axiomatic that our economy is shifting from one driven by industry to one driven by information. For two hundred years we have used paper and paper based documents for recording and communicating information. In the 'information society' most of information will be communicated through computers, networks - wired or unwired. The information will be cheaper, occupies less space and communicated with great speed.

INFORMATION AS A COMMODITY

Some view information as a 'commodity' and use this perception to make a case for regulating its flow just as other commodities are regulated. Apart from providing public services, it has become imperative for the governments to provide precise, concise and upto date information as an input for production, distribution, well- being of the society as well as social upliftment.

INFORMATION LITERACY

Information literacy is the ability to recognize the need for information to solve problems and develop ideas; pose important questions; use a variety of information gathering strategies; locate relevant and appropriate information; assess information for quality, authority, accuracy, and authenticity. It includes the abilities to use the practical and conceptual tools of information technology, to understand, form, format, location, and access methods, how information is situated and produced, research processes, and to format and publishing textual and multimedia formats and to adapt to emerging technologies.

Information literacy consists of skills, strategies, and ways of thinking that are essential to success in a knowledge based economy. It is the ability to find and use information with critical discrimination in order to build knowledge. An information literacy person is a lifelong learner, expert in using complex cognitive processes with diverse technological tools in order to solve problems in personal, social, economic, and political contexts. Butterworth states that, there are three identified advantages of information literacy. Firstly, it is a prerequisite for participative citizenship. Secondly, information literacy is required for the production of new knowledge, on which the future economic success of the country depends. Thirdly, it is needed to solve global problems which threaten the planet and the survival of civilization.

INFORMATION NEEDS

The concept of need can be identified in three forms and the distinction between them is essential to understand present and possible library action. First, the unfelt or unactivated need, is the most difficult form to evaluate but it is not to be ignored. They are affected by environmental factors that help the development of needs. Second, "unexpressed needs, those that people feel or are aware of without using the library as a means to satisfy them, i.e., they are not expressed in a library context." third, intentional and unintentional needs. The felt need which is the one's desire to use the library in connection with some problem or work leads to the international and specific use of the library. The unintentional or general need is the one's general feeling to use the library.

William A. Katz stated a useful categorization of information needs. First category, is social or pragmatic information need. It is the information required to cope with day-to-day life within a geographic community. Second category is recreational information need. It is the information required to satisfy the recreational needs and cultural interests of an individual. Third category is professional information need. It is the information required to operate competently within a business or professional environment. Fourth category is educational information need. It is the information required to satisfy academic requirements at an institution.

INFORMATION LITERATE

Earlier one who can read and write was regarded as 'literate'. But today, there are several sources of information apart from written sources - the media (like TV, radio, newspapers, magazines' the computer (know-how to use and exploit the resources on tapes, discs, Internet, etc.); and increased interaction between individuals and groups (telephone, conferences, peer advice, etc.)

INFORMATION SEEKERS

An informed citizen is an asset to a democratic system of government and the proper utilisation of information can improve the quality of citizens. Further, it stated that one of the main aims of the national library and information policy should be to foster, promote and sustain, by all appropriate means, the organisation, availability and use of information in all sectors of national activity.

COMMUNITY INFORMATION SERVICE (CIS)

Community services have been existing in India since the inception of Gram Panchayats, but the term Community information Service (CIS) is of recent origin and may have its roots in the West. It has been emerging as a fact of public library system in the developing countries; with Britain and America taking the lead in this regard.

The public libraries which are working with a statutory provision should take a lead in India. The Government of India appointed a Committee under the Chairmanship of Prof. D.P. Chattopadhyaya (Chairman, RRRLF) to prepare a draft of National Policy on Library and Information System (NAPLIS). The draft of NAPLIS, submitted to the Government of India in March 1986, has strongly emphasised on the need for provision of information services to citizens.

SERVICES

A developing country like India may concentrate its services to a few thrust areas in the initial stages. Some of the suggested areas are :

Health : immunisation, hospitals, admission procedures, first aid, grandma's remedies;

Education : Courses, colleges, teachers, admission procedures;

Agriculture : new farming methods, seeds, insecticides, fertilizers, etc;

Village industries : assistance for setting up, financial sources, technical know-how;

Utilisation of local resources : human and material;

Transport : bus, rail, etc;

Daily necessities : strong supplying provisions and food grains at reasonable rates;

Sources of finance : banks, governments subsidies, etc;

Redressal of grievances of villagers : contact points, government agencies/Departments.

Government welfare schemes : rural development, weaker sections, etc;

Consumer services;

Housing : and

Schemes mainly intended for most backward areas.

POSITION OF THE LIBRARY

In the new emerging information system, the administrators have to decide whether the library is to be a part of the information system in a village or the library should be the hub of the entire information system of the village. The LIS profession should try to work for radiating all information services at the local level through the library. The Society and the information needs of the users are fast changing and it is time for the libraries to act quickly and prove the role the libraries can play in the 'information society'.

The Kerala Example

Use of Information Technology (IT) for rural development was initiated in 1997. In Ernakulam District which has the distinction of being the first district in the country to achieve 100% literacy was chosen for the IT experiment. Under this project, all the departments at the Panchayat level in 20 selected Panchayats were collected through volunteers and entered in Malayalam using a phonetic key-board. An information network was created at each Panchayat. Now this information base is being used far decentralised planning in vague in Kerala. This scheme is named as the Information Kerala Mission (IKM) and is slated to cover all the 990 Panchayats in the State.

Under this programme a computer with Internet facility is located in the Local Library and is jointly managed by the Panchayat and the Dept. of Information Technology, Govt. of Kerala. The centre is named as "*Sevana*" which provides the following information :

1. Welfare programmes of the government
2. Application farms far various support programmes
3. Information about universities, colleges, schools etc. qualification required, admission procedures, etc., including results;
4. Tourism
5. Electronic telephone directory
6. Public Service Commission information, Employment information
7. Question banks far competitive examinations

8. Career guidance;
9. Air and rail timings etc.

These centres are expected to organize 'awareness' programmes for public.

The library is thus chosen as a nodal point for providing community information in Kerala.

INFORMATION TECHNOLOGY (IT) IN OTHER STATES

Andhra Pradesh : The thrust in IT applications in AP is on e-governance. Computer network is used for recording data of commercial taxes, excise, treasuries, transport, etc, and their application. Hyderabad is connected with all district headquarters enabling videoconferencing facility. Land records have been computerised to a large extent. It has a plan to link all 1125 Mandals in the State. It is proposed to computerise 7.67 crore citizen records, 1.2 crore land records and 1.67 crore household records.

The Duggirala Citizens Information System in AP proved that telecentres can be effectively operated by NGOs.

Karnataka: Karnataka provided leadership in IT in India. There are about 822 software companies exporting IT goods worth 1.2 billion during 1999-2000. It has initiated Grampanchayat Information System (GPIS) in 1999 with a pilot project at Bellandur near Bangalore. It is expected that GPIS will have records of roads, water supply, irrigation, rainfall, etc, vital for planning. This information is to be made accessible to public through the "Gram Panchayat Information Kiosks".

Madhya Pradesh: Though, nearly half of the population is below poverty line in MP, it has taken lead role in taking IT to various parts of the State under its "Gyandoot" (= Internet) Programme. A pilot project was initiated in the Dhar district of MP wherein 311 Gram Panchayats extending over 600 villages covering about 5 lakh population. This intranet link is connected to the Internet. The corresponding Internet web-site is GYANDOOT. NET. This network is providing prices and volumes of local markets, land records, public information, etc. E-mail replies are provided for public queries.

Other States : Almost all states have taken IT initiatives in a big or small way. Thus, the changes are going to be fast and conspicuous. A couple of projects worth mentioning here are "Information Villages Project" in Pondichery initiated by M S Swaminathan Research Foundation and IDRC, Canada; and Warna Wired Village Project implemented by NIC, Pune; Govt. of Maharashtra; and Warna Cooperative Society.

GENERAL INFORMATION SERVICES (GISTNIC)

In this era of information age, right to information has become the order of the day. To collect data about various walks of life, churning them into useful information is a gigantic task. In view of the availability of NICNET throughout the country including all states and districts and with the advent of Internet, reaching the people with information (and vice versa) is no more a dream. The General Information Service Terminal of National Informatics Centre (GISTNIC) is a national project, in meeting the challenge of data collection, moulding it as useful information and making it available on internet for public access.

GISTNIC is designed with an objective to make available the general information to public using the state of the art of technology. The data flows constantly at regular intervals from various sectors such as Agriculture, Corporate Industry, Financial Institutions and so on and the same is being updated regularly on GISTNIC systems. The content and scope of information provided on GISTNIC span a wide range of potential users like farmers, tourists, students, researchers and Government Departments etc. The information requirements of individuals vary widely.

In addition to the information being derived out of the databases maintained for Government applications, a large amount of published and open information which are noteworthy for the common man is also being provided through this service.

GISTNIC project in AP offering a lot of information categorized into the following :

1. Agriculture Statistics
2. Corporate Statistics
3. Primary Census Abstract-91
4. District Profiles
5. Public Finance
6. Education After 10+2
7. Gist-education
8. Gtist-std Codes
9. Rural Technologies
10. Exports Statistics
11. Engineering Admissions
12. Social Sector Statistics
13. Industries Directory
14. Tourism Information
15. Industrial Statistics
16. Traditional Sciences
17. Industry Infrastructure
18. Village Amenities
19. Primary Census Abstract-1991 in Hindi Telugu Tamil
20. Provisional Census-2001 Population Figures for A.P., in Telugu
21. Govt. Orders

22. Marketing
23. Vaidyavidhan Parishad
24. A.P. State Museum
25. Cooperatives
26. Technical Education
27. Directory Of World Government Web Sites

RURAL INFORMATICS

National Informatics Centre (NIC) introduced Information Technology (IT) in Rural Development (RD) sector in the year 1986 and since then the three entities have been going hand in hand leading to the evolution of Rural Informatics in India. It is worth mentioning that induction of IT in Rural Development and its subsequent evolution have not been easy tasks, owing to the unstructured nature of RD domain, slow pace of development reforms, low IT literacy and usual reluctance to adopt IT. Nevertheless, Rural Informatics has reached a stage today where IT finds a significant place in RD, not only in terms of expanse and magnitude of its application but also in terms of technological advancement.

NIC's incessant efforts towards computerisation of RD sector have not only facilitated the planning and monitoring agencies but have also created a foundation for building IT services which are of direct significance to the public.

Following is a windows view of major IT applications across various layers of administrative set-up under the Rural Development sector.

1. Database applications;
2. Web-based applications;
3. Geographical information system applications;
4. Multi-media applications;
5. Training in the use of application software;

6. National level projects, like:
   (i) Computerised Rural Information Systems Project (CRISP);
   (ii) Communication institutes of rural development;
   (iii) Integrated management Information System (IMIS);
   (iv) Rajiv Gandhi National Drinking Water Mission (RGNDWM);
   (v) Land Records computerization (LRC), etc.
7. Taking IT to the masses;
8. 'Rural Soft 2000'
9. Rural Bazar (about products and production);
10. Wired villages - Warana; etc.

ELECTRONIC NETWORKS

Electronic technologies have already had considerable impact. Virtually all libraries are now members of networks that greatly facilitate the location of sources of information and the gaining of access to them.

The wholesale integration of information technology into main stream organisation is considered to be a powerful way of fostering more collaboration and cooperation between individuals, reshaping work-styles and improving communication flows.

Information in electronic form can be several things at once, a multi-media fusion not just of sound, text and image but animation, video-chips, software applications and real time discussion.

Hypertext has brought several new dimensions to the information seeking process by establishing both interactive and non-linear approaches to accessing data.

In special information units the traditional on-line databases and familiar CD-ROM products have been joined by the Internet and World Wide Web (www), electronic journals, group were, e-mail and internet.

New Document Delivery Services, Database access, Internet, Electronic publishing, electronic journals consortia approach made information accessible quickly, in all its ramifications in a cheaper manner.

DEVELOPMENTS IN INDIA

Consortia

Following are some of the latest developments in India:

1. FORSA (forum for Resource sharing in Astronomy);
2. INDEST (Indian Digital Library in Engineering Science and Technology);
3. MM Consortia;
4. IGCAR (Indira Gandhi Centre for Atomic Research) 'Science Direct' with access to Elseviar Journals;
5. UGC'S INFLIBNET initiative;
6. CSIR consortium, etc.

UGC AND INFLIBNET INITIATIVE FOR THE UNIVERSITY SYSTEM (INFONET)

Though the focus of this study is towards Science and Technology libraries in India, one of the consortia models established for the university system in India is discussed here, which has successfully initiated a model for resources subscriptions for their members.

There are 297 universities in India, out of which 150 are assisted by UGC (University Grants Commission) and 142 universities are funded by INFLIBNET.

The initiative of e-resources subscription from UGC and INFLIBNET in the 10th five- year plan is to provide wider and larger access to electronic journals and databases. The basic current journals collection has an average of 250 titles, out of which 60% are Indian publications, as a few universities do not subscribe to any foreign journal.

A model, which is being proposed to satisfy their member libraries include the following points:

1. This model will provide access to and support only electronic version.
2. It is decided no to link this model with print subscription.
3. This model will enable perpetual access to subscribed resources, and archival access for back issues.
4. This model to include few print subscriptions.
5. The subscription to journals commitment for minimum 3 years initially.
6. This commitment to be reviewed at the end of three years.

FUTURE PLAN

It is expected to extend this initiative to other areas, including humanities and social sciences. It is envisaged to include more universities, depending on the active participation and cooperation received from them. The essential issue of support of funding is required from the government and UGC on long-term basis.

This model is in its initial phase of conducting the pilot work for identification of members and resources. If it can be implemented and monitored successfully, it will be a major consortium model with more members and resources in the university system in India.

UGC PLAN TO SET-UP VIRTUAL UNIVERSITY

UGC has mooted a proposal of setting-up a 'virtual varsity' that does away with the need for classrooms. It offers interaction with teachers via television using the EDUSAT satellite and also makes available the study material on the

Internet that can be accessed from home.

Examinations too would be conducted on line for different undergraduate and postgraduate courses.

The proposal by the Consortium for Educational Communication (CRC) an inter- university wing of the UGC comes against the backdrop of a Bill passed by Parliament that mandates increase in number of seats to allow *quotas* for OBCs in government aided educational institutions.

CEC Director G.D. Sharma told "This will facilitate anytime, anywhere learning by the students." "CEC has installed satellite interactive terminal in most of the genual universities across the county where student scan, go and participate in the programmes" be added.

The CEC has also installed 'receive only' terminals in several colleges including 72 institutions in North-East States. The programme initially is not interactive. The programmes on the contents of each of the subjects are under preparation.

CONCLUSION

1. Information literacy (IL) do not warrant traditional literacy.
2. IL is accessibility of information to one and all.
3. IL not only improve the knowledge of the individual, but also contribute for the economic development of the individual and the society at large.
4. Information Technology not only contribute to information literacy but also provide life long, perpetual, self education.
5. IL crosses all boundaries - individual, institution language, region, etc.

22

Use of Modern Management Concepts in Library and Information Centres*

MANAGEMENT

Management is a mental process. Right from the dawn of civilization man has been acquiring and sharpening the principle of management for better understanding of nature, better exploitation of resources, better human relations, better organisation and governance. Scientific management though is of fairly recent origin, it has caught the attention of scientists, planners and policy-framers, officers and decision-makers, and in fact every one in every field. Today

* Keynote Address delivered at the Conference on "Modern Management Techniques in Library and Information Centres in the Electronic Era" held at New Arts, Commerce and Science College, Wardha on 11 December 2012.

management has attained the status of science by seminal contributions of men like Taylor, Frank and Gilbreth, Gantt, Fayol and others. Library and Information profession has started adopting the principles of scientific management for library administration since the middle of the 20th century.

What is Management ?

What Is management? Why today so much emphasis is being given to management in almost every type of organisation? The reason is obvious. Every organisation has its own objectives or goals. It needs some system or too! which can utilise its resources (men, material and money) effectively to achieve these objectives. This system, which leads, guides and directs the organisation to achieve its predetermined objectives is called Management.

It is not that earlier the 'art of management' was not there, in fact, it was there at all the times in different 'forms' in different organisations. The only difference is that this art, system, practice, experience or philosophy was not widely known to the public. This came to light very recently through various communication means when it crossed the barriers of people, organisations, languages and countries to which it was originally confined. Today, these managerial functions and principles are universal and applied to all types of organisations depending upon situation or environment to provide effective results. Libraries and Information Centres are not exception to it.

Definitions

The term management has been defined in several ways. Every writer has tried to define in his own way. Though the nature and function of management has increasingly become dear, yet the experts in the field of management have not given a clear-cut definition of the term. Majority of persons who have tried to define management have really given the functions of management and some of those definitions are given below:

1. Management is a distinct process consisting of planning, organising, actuating, controlling, and utilizing. It is both a science and an art followed in order to accomplish pre-determined objectives
   — *George R Terry*
2. Management is the art of getting things done through and with informally organised group
   — *Harold Koontz*
3. Management is the accomplishment of result through the efforts of other people — *Lawrence Appley*
4. A multipurpose organ that manages a business and manages managers and manages workers and work
   — *Peter F. Drucker*
5. To manage is to forecast, to plan, to organize, to command, to coordinate and to control — *Henri Fayol*
6. Management is the process by which managers create, direct, maintain, and operate purposive organisation through systematic, coordinated, cooperative human effort — *Dalton E. McFarianc*

Nature and Purpose

Management is the process of designing and maintaining an environment in which individuals, working together, in groups, efficiently accomplish selected aims. This basic definition needs to be expanded:

1. As managers, people carry out the managerial functions of planning, organizing, stalling, leading, and controlling.
2. Management applies to any kind of organization.
3. It applies to managers at all organizational levels.
4. The aim of all managers is the same: to create a surplus,
5. Managing is concerned with productivity; this implies effectiveness and efficiency.

Characteristics

There are many other definitions and each one uses the term management in different ways.

What we can derive from the different definitions is the characteristics of management. An analysis of different definitions reveal some of the following features of Management

1. It is an art as well as science-it is an art because managerial skill is a personal possession and intuitive. It is a science because, it has developed certain laws, generalizations which to a great extent universally applicable.
2. It is a process-The executives or managers who utilize the resources to the optimum benefit in the process of management. It involves, the course of action to be taken, securing necessary physical means, recruiting for the performance of requisite tasks, and the process involves to see that the job is properly accomplished.
3. It is a group effort-Management to be successful requires the effort of a group of persons and not any particular individual.
4. Achievement of the objectives : Management presupposes some goals to achieved. There must be predetermined objectives and the group involved should strive to fulfil these objectives,
5. Management is a system of authority-authority is considered as a basic managerial function. It is a rule-enforcing body and is bound with a web of relationship between superiors and subordinates.
6. Management is an entity by itself-Management is a separate and distinct entity. The function of management is how to get the work done, and not necessary for the manager to do himself.

7. Management is needed at all levels-Management is not restricted at the top level only. Even the lowest level supervisor has to perform the same type of function of decision-making as at the top level.

Functions

Many scholars and managers have found that the analysis of management is facilitated by a useful and clear organization of knowledge. In studying management, therefore, it is helpful to break it down into five managerial functions - planning, organizing, staffing, leading, and controlling - around which can be organized the knowledge that underlies those functions. Thus, the concepts, principles, theory, and techniques of management are grouped into these five functions.

This framework has been used and tested for many years. Although there are different ways of organizing managerial knowledge, most textbook authors today have adopted this or a similar framework even after experimenting at times with alternative ways of structuring knowledge.

Some scholars have organized managerial knowledge around the roles of managers, as shown, in the perspective. Indeed, this approach has made some valuable contributions to the study of management, since it also focuses on what managers do and provides evidence of planning, organizing, staffing, leading, and controlling.

Generally, the emphasis is on managers' tasks that pertain to designing an internal environment for performance within an organization. It must never be overlooked that managers must operate in the external environment of an enterprise as well. Clearly, managers cannot perform their tasks well unless they have an understanding of, and are responsive to, the many elements of the external environment—economic, technological, social, political, and ethical factors that effect their areas of operations.

Managers are charged with the responsibility of taking actions that will make it possible for individuals to make their best contributions to group objectives. Management thus applies to small and large organizations, to profit and not-for-profit enterprises, to manufacturing as well as service! industries. The term "enterprise" refers to businesses, government agencies, hospitals, universities, and other organizations, since almost everything said here refers to business as well as non-business organizations. Effective managing is the concern of the corporation president, the hospital administrator, the government, first-line supervisor, the Boy Scout leader, the Bishop in the church, the baseball manager, and the university president.

MANAGERIAL FUNCTIONS AT DIFFERENT ORGANISATIONAL LEVELS

Generally, no distinction is made between managers, executives, administrators, and supervisors. To be sure, a given situation may differ considerably among various levels in an organization or various types of enterprises. Similarly, the scope of authority held may vary and the type of problems dealt with may be considerably different. Furthermore, the person in a managerial role may be directing people in the sales, engineering, or finance department. But the fact remains that, as managers, all obtain results by establishing an environment for effective group endeavour.

All managers carry out managerial functions. However, the time spent for each functions may differ. Top-level managers spend more time on planning and organizing than do lower-level managers. Leaders on the other hand, takes a great deal of time for first-line supervisors. The difference in the amount of time spent on controlling varies only slightly for managers at various levels.

Managerial Roles

The ten managerial roles identified by Minfeberg are:

Interpersonal Roles

1. The figure head role (performing ceremonial and social duties as the organization's representative).
2. The leader role.
3. The liaison role (communicating particularly with outsiders).

Informational Roles

1. The recipient role (receiving information about the operation of an enterprise).
2. The disseminator role (passing information to subordinates).
3. The spokesperson role (transmitting information to those outside the organization).

Decision Roles

1. The entrepreneurial role.
2. The disturbance-handler role.
3. The resource allocator role.
4. The negotiator role (dealing with various persons and groups of persons).

Management Skills

Robert L. Katz identified three kinds of skills for administrators. To these maybe added a fourth the ability to design solutions.

1. *Technical skill* is knowledge of and proficiency in activities involving methods, processes, and procedures. Thus, it involves working with tools and specific techniques. For example, mechanics work with tools, and their supervisors should have the ability to teach them how to use these tools. Similarly,

accountants apply specific techniques in doing their job.

2. *Human skill* is the ability to work with people; it is cooperative effort; it is teamwork; it is the creation of an environment in which people feel secure and free to express their opinions.
3. *Conceptual skill* is the ability to see the "big picture," to recognize significant elements in a situation, and to understand the relationships among the elements.
4. *Design skill* is the ability to solve problems in ways that will benefit the enterprise. To be effective particularly at upper organizational levels, managers must be able to do more than see a problem. They must have, in addition, the skill of a good design engineer in working out a practical solution to a problem. If managers merely see the problem and become "problem watchers," they will fail. Managers must also have that valuable skill of being able to design a workable solution to the problem in the light of the realities they face.

STRATEGIC MANAGEMENT

Strategic management is the key to successful development of services in the information sector as much as in any other.

Kinnel Evans says that strategic management differs from some other aspects of management in its concern for the whole organization and the direction in which it will travel; other types of management activity are essentially concerned with the effective operation of various functions to improve efficiency. A strategic approach to management is externally focused; and internal operations are considered primarily in relation to the positioning of the organization with regard to competitors and profitability—in the case of public sector organizations, survivability and resource acquisition are of key importance. Strategic management involves analysing the current position of the organization, generating and choosing possible alternative courses of action, matching these to the resource capabilities of the organization and then planning the implementation and review of the chosen strategy.

According to Hayes, strategic management is that part of the general management of organizations that emphasizes the relationships to external environments, evaluates the current status and the effects of future changes in them, and determines the most appropriate organizational response.

Key Concepts

According to Armstrong, the key concepts in strategic management are:

- Distinctive competence (what the organization is good at and what special or unique capabilities it has)
- Focus (concentration on strategic issues)
- Competitive advantage (the targeting of markets where its competences give it an edge)
- Synergy (the abilities and skills of people throughout the organization contribute to problem-solving and strategy development)
- Environmental scanning (examination of the internal and external environment, to be aware of strengths and weaknesses, threats and opportunities)
- Resource allocation (ensuring that human, financial, plant and equipment resources are available, and that, their use is optimized).

Heeks and Kinnell see strategy as emerging 'from a range of complex interrelationships and responses to environmental factors, rather than being a precisely articulated and co-ordinated process'; it may have high-risk, long-term implications for viability, but will determine survival and direction in the medium term. They identify three steps which comprise strategic management: strategic analysis, strategic choice, and strategic implementation. Values, expectations and objectives fall into the first step; this leads to the generation of options which fall in to the second step; and resource planning is added to complete the process.

Four points are made by Carr in the definition of strategic management.

- Identification of social, technical, economic, political, and structural environments.
- Identification of constraints
- Prioritization
- Monitoring.

These could be applied in the context of customer use, definitions of products or services, skills (that is, human resource development), objectives, and resources. The outcomes foreseen could be judged by usage levels, education of users/non-users, increased value in the organization, and changed perceptions.

The key issues listed by Johnson are finance, IT, stock provision, staff, client groups and marketing. She points out that strategic issues should not be confused with goals and objectives thus causing incomplete descriptions and failures to see inter-relationships.

SOURCES USED

1. Armstrong, M. Management Process and Functions. London: Instt. of Personnel Mgt., 1990.
2. Carr, S.J., Strategic management in libraries, etc. (*Lib. Mgt* v. 13, N5. pp. 4-17).
3. Hayes, R.M. Strategic management for academic libs: A Handbook. Westport: Green wood, 1993.

4. Heeks, P. and Kinnell, M. Managing change for lib services. London: British Lib, 1992,

5. Johnson, H. Strategic planning for modem libraries. (*Lib Magt*, v. 10, Ml. pp. 7-18).

6. Katz, Robert L. Skills of an effective administrator (*Honvard Business Rev*, Jan.-Feb. 1955. pp. 33-42),

7. Koontz, H. and others. Management. Ed7. Mcgraw Hill, 1981.

8. Koontz. Harold and Weihrich, Heinz. Essentials of mgt. Ed5. Delhi: Tata-Mcgraw Hill, 1998..

9. Mittal, RL. Library administration: Theory and practice Ed4, Delhi; Metropolitan, 1978.

10. Mookherjee R.S. and Sengupta, B. Library organisation and administration. Ed2. Calcutta: World Press, 1977.

11. Prytherch, Ray. Strategic management in Author's. Handbook of Lib and Info Mgt. Hants: Gower, 1998.

12. Sharma, J.S. Library Organization. Delhi: Vikas, 1978.

23

Quality in Library Services*

INNOVATION

Innovation is introducing or using new ideas, techniques, etc in order to improve quality or to make progress. Innovation is intrinsic to persons having a passion for quality and betterment. Innovation is individual oriented. Not all have the innovative abilities. Thus quality can be brought in by innovation or adopting best practices

The overall objective of professional is to improve the quality of services by ushering in change in the existing system and services.

CHANGES

The first step in the management of change is to feel the need for change, which is defined by the organization's

---

* Keynote Address delivered at the Conference on "Innovative Best Practices in Library and Information Services" held at LRT Commerce College, Akola on 18 December 2009.

desire to move from the existing situation to the desired situation.

For perceiving a situation for change the managers (here LIS personnel) should constantly scan the internal and external environment; find out probable threats and opportunities, link them with the organization's strengths and weaknesses (i.e. carry out the SWOT analysis); and review current performance periodically and if necessary modify the existing organization structure and policies.

Once the existing situation is analyzed and the need for change is determined, LIS professionals should draw a plan for initiating a change in the organizational structure, new policies, procedures, standards, services, etc.

The plan should be put on a trial-run and only when it is proved to be successful, then only it should be employed in the library. Some times we may come across resistance from staff as well as users to change. Librarians should make all attempts to over come such resistance. Once the resistance is overcome people will accept the change with enthusiasm and willingness. Once the change is implemented it should be monitored and reviewed continuously.

Planning Change in Libraries

This is a complex business but it is increasingly becoming central to management itself. In the context of quality management, change is both internally generated and externally imposed. Quality management itself is concerned with change, with doing things better, more accurately, more consistently, and more appropriately. But it is also concerned with introducing change as a response to the external environment, both in response to the development of customers requirements (and the requirements of new customers) and in exploiting opportunities presented by the environment, for example to reduce the cost of inputs. Change, then is at the centre of quality management.

In recent years the management of change has received considerable attention from practitioners and researchers. A useful practical guide by Curzon (1989), designed for librarians, suggests that a sequence of steps can be sued to plan, implement and evaluate change:

1. **Conceptualizing :** developing awareness and envisioning the change.
2. **Preparing :** getting the organization ready for change, for example by listening to staff but being committed to the change.
3. **Organizing the planning group :** selecting staff to participate and building them into a team.
4. **Planning :** examining options, deciding on goals and objectives and then developing a plan.
5. **Deciding :** evaluating the options, deliberating and then making a decision.
6. **Managing the individual :** discussing the change and dealing with reactions to it, then monitoring its implementation.
7. **Controlling resistance :** identifying resistance, anglicizing its source and counteracting it.
8. **Implementing :** formal introduction of the change at the right time and then following it through.
9. **Evaluating :** re-examining the goals, identifying problems, and making adjustments.

In many ways this scheme is oversimplified of course. In practice there are a number of changes taking place simultaneously and the process will not always follow through a series of identifiable, discrete steps in a neat and and tidy fashion. Nevertheless it recognizes that change does not- or should not- merely happen, and that it has to be managed.

Issues which need to be considered in the management

of change include the political and social context, resource availability and management style. Above all, however, change is dependent on people, on encouraging, persuading and enabling individuals to pursue purposeful change and improve the quality of their own output, whether as part of the internal quality chain or as direct products and service to end users.

QUALITY

Quality means to meet or exceed the needs and expectations of the user in the most cost-effective way. It has 4 basic elements: 1 The user; 2 Cost; 3 Technology; and 4 Viability. Quality in the context of libraries is a measure of achievement of a library in terms of 'User satisfaction'.

The definition of quality given by ISO 9000 is that: ' The totality of features and characteristics of a product or service that bear upon its ability to satisfy stated or implied needs'.

Quality Management

Quality Management is concerned with integration of all efforts in the organization towards quality and customer care. "Quality management represents a customer oriented and quality focused management philosophy."

Quality for Libraries

Gervin identified eight dimensions which characterize a quality service for the customer. These are:

1. Performance : It is pertained to primary operating dimensions of the service. *Ex*. Books, access to databases, access to subject experts, place to sit and work and so on.

2. Secondary Features : Such of these are not essential, but add comfort and convenience to users. *Ex*. easy furniture, provision of a lift, etc.

3. Reliability : Users place high value to reliability or a product *of* service. *Ex*.: A working photocopier service.

4. Conformance : The question here is whether the product or service meets the agreed standard. The service standards for libraries are now starting to emerge.

5. Durability : The normal definition of durability is the amount of use the product will provide before it deteriorates to the point where replacement or discard is preferable to repair. It may be appropriate to consider the age of the library's book stock or the frequency of update of a CD- ROM database.

6. Serviceability : When things go wrong, they should be put to right. The question here is 'how quickly they can be repaired?'. We have also to consider the amount of inconvenience the user will be put to what would be the cost of repair?

7. Aesthetics play an important role in the library. Is the service area is clean and well designed? It is welcoming; does it appear user friendly? all the user judge a library as much by its aesthetics as by its services.

8. Quality Management in Libraries : Quality of service should be enhanced up to the mark of the customer expectation or satisfaction. Quality management involves implementation of quality policy which means quality planning, quality control, quality assurance, and quality improvement within the quality system.

Benefits of Quality Management in Libraries

According to Miller and Steams, the principles of quality management, if implemented carefully would yield immense benefits to a library and information center. They are :

- Incremental changes leading to continuous improvement.
- Forces library managers to develop leadership skill to obtain effective results.

- Increases staff participation in decision making.
- Improves the level of training given to staff, thus increasing their skills and abilities.
- Helps to break down barriers between library sections and improves communication within the organization.
- The time taken to provide information services decreases and the efficiency increases.

Measuring the Quality

The purpose of measuring the quality is to determine the effectiveness, efficiency and value of what have been achieved. This process reveals the strength as well as the weakness of any library or information system.

Different Approaches

1. Complaints and suggestions received from users;
2. Users survey;
3. Bench Marking (Comparing with other functionaries);
4. Establishing quality as a strategic issue;
5. Redefine ring organizational structure;
6. Empowering staff to analyze and solve problems

ROLE OF AICTE NBA IN QUALITY ASSURANCE

National Board of Accreditation (NBM) was set up by AICTE in Sept, 1994 in order to assess the qualitative competence of educational institutions from the Diploma level to the post graduate level in engineering and technology, management and related disciplines.

The NBM aims to bring standards of some of the programs offered in technical institutions on par with programs offered in institutions across USA and Europe, by introducing a quality auditing systems and establishing a datum for measuring the quality and excellence in engineering education. The NBA periodically conducts evaluation of technical institutions and programs on the basis of guidelines, norms and standards specified by the Board.

Suggestions to Enhance Quality

Working hours and Working Days : The library should remain open after the normal college hours and on holidays which will enable to students to use the library services without disturbing their attendance in the class and other teaching-learning activities.

Automation of Library : In the technological era to give services to a technologist in a technical institution without full automation is a thing which can not be thought off. Hence to attract the students each and every activity of the library should be fully automated.

Linking to other Networks : The library should have been interconnected with other systems of similar activities.

E-resource : In addition to the conventional materials, e-resources should occupy a major portion of the space in the stacking area. Documents related to reasoning, aptitude, personality development, English etc. should be available with sufficient copies.

Periodicals : Printed as well as on-line periodicals should be available in the library.

Other Facilities : Facilities like Xeroxing, Internet after college working hours and in holidays, inter-library loan, uninterrupted power supply etc. should be in the list of regular services in the library.

Extension Activities : As per AICTE norms the reading room capacity should be ¼ of intake which indirectly mean that the daily visitors in the library should be more than that. To motivate the students to use the library, extension activities should be a regular feature.

Refresher Course/Carrier Advancement Programmes: Best service can be possible only when the staff in the library is well trained with the latest technology. Hence staff of the library should be encouraged to go through refresher course / carrier advancement programme at regular interval.

Feedback : A positive approach towards the feedback from users can improve the services in the library. As keeping the users satisfied is the main objective of quality assurance.

BEST PRACTICES FOR UNIVERSITY AND COLLEGE LIBRARIES

National Accreditation and Assessment Council (NAAC)

The National Accreditation and Assessment Council (NAAC) strives for quality and excellence in higher education, and advocates for enhancing the role of library and information services in improving the academic environment. In today's high-tech learning environment, the library as a learning resource is taking up increasingly more academic space and time in the life of a learner. Thus, the NAAC has identified the set of best practices in library and information services, with the help of a few case presentations from a few selected libraries of the accredited universities and colleges. A best practice may be innovative, and be a philosophy, policy, strategy, program, process or practice that solves a problem, or create new opportunities. The data on Best Practices have been collected on a format developed by the NAAC and are presented under the four broad areas. (NAAC, BPS, 2006) :

1. Management and Administration of a Library
2. Collection and services
3. Extent of use of services
4. Use of technology

1. Management and Administration of a Library: Identification and internalization of best practices in the management and administrative functions at regular intervals would enhance the collection development process, services and dissemination and use of the library as a whole. (BPS, P 3-15)

2. Collection and Services : A well defined collection development policy that ensures access to peer-reviewed journals procured by individual institutions and a consortia approach as well as networked access to documents of all types available in other academic libraries through inter-institutional cooperation (BPS, P 17-24)

3. Extent of use of services : Continuous user promotion and information literacy programs with novel ideas to enhance the use of library services. User education and use measurement practices are essential for academic libraries to be graded as a best practice.

4. Use of Information Technology : Information technology tools are to be used and constantly updated in libraries. Libraries are encouraged to help in adding value to the existing practices or add new practices that they are adopting for the end user benefit in providing new and improved services.(BPS. P37-59)

CONCLUSION

Change is a way of life whether it is of the individual or institution. Change should bring-in new an innovative ideas and practices in library and information services. Change is noticed at the level of the library and information center as well as at the national and global level. A positive mind for change and adoption of new techniques will bring in a sea of change in library and information services. Change should not be for mere change for all new services being introduced user should be pivotal. Quality in products and services should be the hall-mark of all library services.

REFERENCES

1. Brophy, Peter and Coulling, Kate, Quality management for information and library managers, London: Aslib/Gower,

2. Kumar, PSG, Management of libraries and information centers, New Delhi: BRPC, 2003

3. Natarajan, R, Range of issues relevant to quality and accreditation in engineering education (*Indian Journal of technical Education* v26, n2 ; 2003)

4. NAAC, guideline on quality indicators in library and information Services; universes autonomous college Banglore : NAAC, 2005 2-4

5. Premchand, P. Quality library management for quality library service- Need of the hour (APLA national conference on Re-orientation of library services in India, Vijaywada: APLA, 2007).

24

Innovation as a Tool for Change in Libraries*

INVENTION VIS-A-VIS DISCOVERY

Finding a natural phenomenon, for the first time is described as 'Discovery'. 'Lightening [in the sky] is electricity by Franklin is discovery. But electric bulb developed by Thomas Alva Edison is an invention

Discovery and invention play an important part in any field. So is the case in libraries and information centers. Research forms the basis for either discovery or invention. By and large inventions are based on applied research. Where as, discoveries, are based on observational research. Applied and developmental researches have a powerful, and far-reaching impact.

* Keynote Address delivered at the Seminar on "Innovative Practices in the Management of Library and Information Services" at National Institute of Social Work, Nagpur, on 9 Oct. 2010.

INNOVATION

Innovation is a universal phenomenon. Innovation has a sway on all aspects of the society. Innovative phenomena bring rapid developments in the society. There developments pose new problems. New problems need new solutions. New solutions warrant new research Thus, new research may stir-up existing disciplines and their course of development. Library and information science is no exception to this process.

IMPACT OF INNOVATIONS ON LIBRARIES

Innovations in various fields of human activity will have their own impact on libraries and information centers. L & IC have to reorient their services taking the best advantage of the new innovative practices that already had an indelible impact on the society.

For this purpose, the discipline Library and Information Science should develop suitable mechanisms, systems and services to provide best possible services to the users.

Librarians at local level should also develop innovative methods best suited to their immediate clientele.

- The phenomena of innovation of innovation is not static. It is dynamic, infinite and a continuum.
- It is not a phenomenon of high-end research.
- It has to be developed at various levels.
- It is a not only technology oriented; but also, to be intellectually exercised.
- Every professional is capable of innovation. He should atune his/her mind in that direction.

CONCEPT OF LIBRARY 2.0

The concept of library 2.0 is a classical example of

innovation in libraries. The principles of web 2.0 have been ingeniously adopted for vitalizing library services.

WEB TECHNOLOGY

Web 2.0 represents an environment where communities of participants with common interests contributes to a collective intelligence, and where dynamic, hardware independent applications can be developed with the help of users. Web 2.0 features include blogs, pod casts, share news social networking Wikis, and other technology-based capabilities that allow users business, or individuals to connect with and learn from each other.

Web 2.0 is used to describe the emerging Internet technologies and the birth of Library 2.0 is the use of these new web applications within the library system. Traditionally, we were locked our resources behind passwords and barcodes, keeping things in catalogues and databases so no one could access except those coming to the sites to do manual searches. Feedback is always solicited from the users. Library 2.0 has emerged as using new web technologies to connect and establish relationship with patrons. The basic idea of Library 2.0 is to transform library services by making them more personalized and more web-based along with web 2.0 lines.

Today's web sites are now dynamic rather than being static, web sites have become platforms for web applications for end users. With the use of development systems such as AJAX (Asynchronous Java Script and XML), their applications, for example word processing, spreadsheets and slide show presentations. These are applications that the general public is familiar with, making it easier for an end user to operate. These new web applications are often much more complicated to design and lead to creating employment opportunities for it professionals. The way in which communities interact has changed with 2.0 innovations. No longer do people depend on written letters in the post or telephone calls to communicate. Web 2.0 has helped to create online social networks for public use; some of them provide social software that members can use to connect with each other.

WEB 2.0

Web 2.0 refers to a perceived second generation of web based communities and hosted services such as social net sites wikis and folksonomics which aim to facilitate collaboration and sharing between the users " web 2.0'" first used by O'Reilly Media as the name of a services of web developed Conferences (www.web2.0con.com) that started in 2004. Sub-categories of what web 2.0 encapsulates include usability, economy, participation, convergence design, standardization and remix ability. These categories are further broken down with sub categories such as blogs, audio, video, RSS,open APIS , wikis. Social software and focus on simplicity. Tim O'Kelly also describes web 2.0 as the business revolution in the computer industry caused by the move to the Internet as platform and an attempt to understand the rules of success on that new platform.

A general comparison between web2.0 and web 1.0 is shown in Table 1.

Table 1. Difference between web 1.0 and 2.0

	Web 1.0	Web 2.0
Mode of usage	Read	Write and contribute
Unit of content	Page	Record
How content is viewed	Web browser	Browser, RSS readers, Mobile devices, etc.
Creation of content	By web site authors	By everyone

The use of hyper linking on web pages underpins the on web page underpins the 2.0 web. The high level of connect-ability between content on the web has encouraged sustained growth as more and more users add new content. Users can then link to newly discovered sites in a way similar to dendrites forming relationship in the human brain. The success of Google is a result of 2.0 technologies. Google have created a business from linking users of one site to the information or services provided by another. Google has none of the trappings of software provider's products. These trappings are the purchase cost of the software, limited applications to a particular platform and the product life span where the next generation would involve the consumer having to purchase an upgrade or a whole new software package. A lot of the people involved in the development of web 1.0 are today involved in the web 2.0 industry; this bank of knowledge can only help guarantee the success of web 2.0 applications. In web 1.0 many companies which were involved in the original 'dot com' era had moved on to join larger companies. This suggests that there is plenty of web experience in the mix. These people will have the knowledge of what works and what doesn't. But more importantly, why something does or does not work.

Today's web sites are now dynamic rather than being static. Web sites have become platforms for web applications for end users. With the use of development systems such as AJAX (Asynchronous Java Script and XML), their applications, for example word processing, spreadsheets and slide show presentations. These are applications that the general public is familiar with, making it easier for an end user to operate these applications. These new web applications are often much more complicated to design and create, creating employment opportunities for it professionals. The way in which communities interact has changed with 2.0 innovations. No longer do people depend on written letters in the post or telephone calls to communicate. Web 2.0 has helped to create online social networks for public use; some of them provide social software that members can use to connect with each other.

WEB 2.0 TECHNOLOGIES

The web 2.0 technologies include:

1. **Blogs :** Blogs are on-line journals or diaries hosted on a web site and often distributed to other sites or readers using RSS (Really simple Syndication)

2. **Collective intelligence :** This refers to any system that attempts to tap the expertise of a group rather than an individual to make decisions. Technologies that contribute to collective intelligence include collaborative publishing and common databases for sharing knowledge.

3. **Mash-up :** Mash-ups are aggregations of content from different on-line sources to create a new service. An example would be a program that pulls apartment listings from one site and displays them on a Google map to show where the apartments are located.

4. **Peer to peer Networking (P2P) :** This is a technique for efficiently sharing files

5. **Audio, videos or text :** Either over the internet, or with in a closed set of users. Unlike traditional method of storing a file on one machine, which can become a bottleneck if many people try to access it once-P2P distributes files across many machines, often those of the users themselves. Some systems retrieve files by gathering and assembling pieces of them from many machines.

6. **Podcasts :** They are audio or video recordings, a multi-media form of a blog, or other content. They are often distributed through an aggregator.

7. **RSS (Really Simple Syndication) :** RSS allows people to subscribe to on-line distributions of news, blogs, pod casts, or other information.

8. Social Networking : It refers to systems that allow members of a specific site to learn about other member's skills, talents, knowledge, or preference. Commercial examples include Facebook and Linkedln. Some companies use these systems internally to identify experts.

9. Web-Services : Web-services are software systems that make it easier for different systems to communicate with one another automatically in order to pass information or conduct transactions. For example, a retailer, and supplier might use web services to communicate over the Internet and automatically update each other inventory systems.

10. Wikis : Such as *Wikipedia* is system for collaborative publishing. They allow many authors to contribute to an on-line document or discussion.

This new approach makes it possible for searchers to be presented with choices to view on-line, borrow locally, request from other, buy or sell as appropriate to their needs and circumstances.

Library 2.0

According to Miller (2005), 'Library 2.0' is a term coined by Michael Casey on his Libra Crunch blog. Though his writings on Library 2.0 are groundbreaking and in many ways authoritative, Casey (2006) defines the term very broadly, arguing it applies beyond technological innovation and service. He defines 'Library 2.0' as 'the application of interactive, collaborative, and multi-media web-based technologies to web- based library services and collections,' and suggests this definition be adopted by the library science community. Limiting the definition to web-based services, and not library services more generally , avoids potential confusion and sufficiently allows the term to be researched, further theorized, and renders it more useful in professional discourse.

Four Elements of Library 2.0

A theory for Library 2.0 could be understood to have these four essential elements:

It is user-centered

Users participate in the creation of the content and "services they view within the library's web-presence, OPAC etc. The consumption and creation is dynamic, and thus the roles of librarian and user is not always clear.

It Provides a Multi-media Experience

Both the collections and services of Library 2.0 contain video and audio components. While this is not often cited as a function of library 2.0, it is here suggested that it should be.

It is Socially Rich

The library's web-presence includes user's presences. There are both Synchronous (e.g. IM) and asynchronous (e.g. wikis) ways for users to communicate with one another and with librarians.

It is Communally Innovative

This is perhaps the single most important aspect of Library 2.0. It rests on the foundation of libraries as a community service, but understands that as communities change, libraries must not only change with them, and they must allow users to change the library. It seeks to continually change its services, to find new ways to allow communities, not just individual to seek, find, and utilize information.

Library 2.0 is a user-centered virtual community. It is a socially rich, often egalitarian electronic space. While librarian 2.0 might act as a facilitator and provide support, he or she is not necessarily primarily responsible for the creation of the content. Users interact with and create resources with one another and with librarian's In some ways; it is a virtual reality for libraries, a web manifestation of the library as place. A library's presence on the web in library 2.0 includes the presence of that library's constituency and utilizes the same applications and technologies as its community. Habib (2006) recognizes it a very useful model for Library 2.0 with regard to academic libraries.'

Library 1.0 vis-a-vis Library 2.0

Library 2.0 is not about searching, but finding, not about access but sharing. It recognizes that human beings do not seek, and utilize information as individuals, but as communities.

Following are examples of the move from library 1.0 Library 2.0

Library 1.0	Library 2.0
1. E-mail reference/Q&A	1. Chat reference
2. Text-based tutorials	2. Streaming media tutorials with interactive databases
3. E-mail mailing list, web masters	3. Blogs, wikis, RSS feeds
4. Controlled classification schemes	4. Tag 4. Tagging coupled with controlled schemes
5. OPAC	5. Personalized social network interface
6. Catalogue of largely reliable print and electronic holdings	6. Catalogue of reliable and suspect web pages, blogs, wikis etc.

Users' demands are rapidly increasing with the passage of time. The users' approaches are likely transforming staffing levels, services models, access to resources and services etc. Users' are seeking more effective ways of delivered services along with achieving greater returns and undoubtedly libraries have striving to provide the required services to the users. Users require any piece of information irrespective of time and place, and that too on a single platform.

MANAGERIAL CONSIDERATIONS

Before instituting information services in a Library and Information Centre, it is absolutely necessary to consider the following managerial aspects:

1. Feasibility study - to establish the need for and the possibility of instituting information services.
2. Phases of development and services

   Start up costs (initial costs)

   Operational recurring costs

   Effect of the number of users, diversity of services; operational cost—Reimbursable and non-reimbursable costs

   Ease in terms of available resources-information sources, personnel facilities, equipment, materials and operation

   Length of startup time

   Training of personnel required

   Extent of derangement of existing organizational structure, displacement of personnel, etc.

PATTERN OF SERVICES

The variety of services provided by a Library and Information Centre follows a basic pattern. On the basis of the pattern chosen, certain mechanisms are adopted which help in the designing and development of certain matching services. Some of the basic mechanisms (processes/techniques) and the corresponding services, discernible in any Library and Information Centre are:

1. Reference/Referral Mechanism : Reference Services

2. Announcement Mechanism : Current Awareness Services

3. Accretion Mechanism : Indexing and Abstracting services

4. Evaluation Mechanism : State of the art report/Trend Report Service, Critical Compilations and Reviews, etc.

5. Document Access Mechanism : Reprographic and Translation Services

6. Promotion/Liaison Mechanism : Liaison Services, Technical Enquiry Services

It is essential to note that the first four mechanisms generate information services. The fifth and sixth mechanisms generate supporting services which help in the dissemination of information.

It may be noted that each group of services/products forms the input for subsequent activities and products.

25
Technical / Report Writing*

TECHNICAL / REPORT WRITING—WHAT?

Research and development reports have emerged as a distinctive form of literature brought out by various technical and academic institutions. The results of research add to the fountain of knowledge and permit their use as a basis for action. In business or industry also, an orderly presentation of facts about a specific activity or programme is useful.

Why ?

A 'Report' is a document in which a given problem is examined in some detail. The effectiveness of a report greatly depends on the clarity and completeness of the contents and presentation. Report writing is functional writing. The ABC of functional writings is-Accuracy, Brevity and Clarity. A report must convey facts based on findings by observation,

* Text of the Lecture delivered at the Workshop Organised by the Deptt. of Library and Information Science, RTM Nagpur University, Nagpur on 3 Dec. 2009.

experimentation or research), spell out ideas and make recommendations.

Every report sees four stages: 1. Presentation; 2. Arrangement; 3. Writing and 4. Revision.

How ?

Before proceeding to write one must make it clear in mind about the subject, scope and purpose. Decide for what purpose you are writing? Are you trying to introduce a new idea? Are you reporting some findings or, recommending a course of action?

Ask Yourself: Who is my reader? What is his background knowledge? What is his technical level? What is his level of understanding? What additional knowledge is to be provided? What details are to be given? etc.

Arrangement

The information is to be presented in a logical sequence. The arrangement of information is to be decided on the basis of answers to the subject matter? What terminology and what kind of words are to be used? What ideas are to be emphasized? How the text is to be substantiated by tables, charts, diagrams, illustrations, etc?

Writing

Before start writing, satisfy yourself whether you study has met the objectives aimed at. That, your study or the results of your study has some social and scientific significance.

Remember that you are writing a functional report. Bombast, verbal stroke-play and purple passages do not have a place in it. A clear business - like and balanced style is best.

The language should be terse with words used economically; selected avoiding words with overtones and undertones and with one to one meaning.

Put the material in the sequence planned earlier. The first draft is always a rough draft, which will require revision and polishing. If possible, write the first draft in one sitting which will give a uniform and flowing style.

The title of the report should be comprehensive and concise giving a complete understanding of the contents. Introduction should spell out the background of the work, earlier studies, objectives, methodology, hypothesis, equipment used and if possible a glossary of terms used in the text. Conclusion should give a brief account of main discussion, findings and inferences, recommendations and areas of further research or follow - up action to be taken.

Revision

When you have completed the draft of your report, have it out of sight for a week or two and then try to re-read it with a fresh mind. "Write in haste and polish at leisure" is a good principle to follow. Cut and change to get the meaning clear.

EDITING

What ?

Editing is an essential step in improving the quality of the report in terms of presentation, grammar, typography and format, balance in contents, etc.

Why ?

Errors from many sources creep into manuscripts and reports. The editor is the chief check against them. Since, even a well written manuscript can be bettered. Editor should aim at presenting the manuscript in its most appetizing form, phraseology and true spirit to the reader.

How?

The editor should see that the manuscript meets certain standards with regard to contents, organization, style and format. The editor should not only correct the errors, but also try to improve it. The edited report should be concise (use fewest words to convey the most meaning); forceful (is being effective in communication); clear (with no fog); and complete (with background, present work, indicating course of action etc.) as detailed earlier.

The job of editing can be of two kinds-*Mechanical editing,* which seeks to correct punctuation, spelling and grammar; and *substantive editing,* wherein editor will also look into the meaning, rewriting or reorganizing if necessary and polishing the author's usage and language without changing original style of the author.

AREAS

Typography and Format

The editor should carefully check title, sub-title, author's name, qualification, references, notes sectional heading, typography, illustrations, appendices, quotations, numbers, dates, proper names, pagination, continuity of text, etc.

Preparation

The editor should also pay attention to the *Language and its use* -with simple sentences, no slang, understandable jargon, no cliche (over using a hackneyed phrase); Grammar - Covering number and active verbs, sequence of tense, avoiding split infinitives, use of active voice over passive voice, avoiding pronouns as far as possible; *Spelling*-American or British (we mostly use the British in India), capitalization, hyphenating, abbreviations, use of foreign words, proper names, etc; *Style* - Uniformity with easy flow; *facts*- to be checked and rechecked; *sense* - Sequence, logic in writing, clear in suggestions; and *editing* - with clear conclusions, specific recommendations and suggestions.

PRINTING AND PROOF READING

Proof Reading

After editing the manuscript is sent to the printer. The editor uses certain standard symbols to mark the changes he wants, which are generally known to the printer. After the matter is composed, it should be read once against to detect mistakes that might have occurred in composing. This is known as proof - reading. A proof - reader uses the same symbols used by the editor to instruct corrections. A proof reader generally takes care of typographical errors, punctuation marks, numbering, pagination, wrong typefaces, missing letters, etc.

Printing

Three kinds of typographic printing can be distinguished: Letter Press, Gravure and Lithography. Letter press printing is still largely used method of printing books, periodicals, newspapers, etc. Gravure printing is used mainly for reproducing art illustrations. Lithogrpahy is used mostly for printing maps, posters, etc.

Office Reproduction

There are a variety of typographic printing processes broadly termed as "office reproduction techniques." These include non-composition master production flat-bed offset, stencil and spirit duplicating, as well as advanced methods of editorial document processing. Electronic typewriters provide variety of type sizes, sets of types and styles of type faces; which closely resemble print type. They permit differential spacing line justification, etc. The Vari-typer is specially used for complex scientific and technical texts. The flexowriter produces both a typescript copy which can be used for the preparation of a printing master, and a punched paper tape which can be used for the second-automatic-retyping of the composed text and can also serve as input to a computer.

Photo-Typesetting

Like composing typewriters, phototypesetting machines have been increasingly used for the preparation of printing masters. These machines use a variety of type-faces styles and signs of different alphabets and have great potentialities for changing type size. The trend is toward highspeed electronic printing devices permitting a direct output of textual and graphical information from computers.

Desk-Top Publishing (DTP)

DTP is a combination of page make-up software running on a computer with a laser printer for the production of copy. DTP is used for preparation of documents such as reports, newsletters, leaflets, posters, manual, brochures and invoices which contain text and often graphics, where presentation is important.

DTP packages arrived in mid-1980s and were more sophisticated than word-processing packages at that time. The present word-processing packages have most of the features of DTP package. Generally documents are created and edited in word-processing packages and then imported into the DTP package, where the pages are designed. Desk-Top CD-ROM publishing is a new area of development.

SOURCES USED

1. Atherton, Pauline A. Handbook for information Systems and Services. Paris:Unesco, 1977 pp. 188-89
2. Carter, Roger. Information Technology Handbook. London: Heinemann, 1987.
3. Feinstein, David L. and others. Computers: Concepts and application, Ed.4. WmC. Brown, 1990.
4. Koul, R. Abacus to artificial intelligence.(*Sc. Reporter* v 25; June 1988.p. 320-25).